AMAZING WORLD WAR II STORIES

THE UNBREAKABLE ZAMPERINI

A WORLD WAR II SURVIVOR'S BRAVE STORY

by Nel Yomtov
illustrated by Rafal Szlapa

Consultant:
Tim Solie
Adjunct Professor of History
Minnesota State University, Mankato
Mankato, Minnesota

CAPSTONE PRESS
a capstone imprint

Graphic Library is published by Capstone Press,
1710 Roe Crest Drive, North Mankato, Minnesota 56003
www.capstonepub.com

Library of Congress Cataloging-in-Publication data
Names: Yomtov, Nelson, author. | Szlapa, Rafal, illustrator.
Title: The unbreakable Zamperini : a World War II survivor's brave story / by Nel Yomtov ;
   illustrated by Rafal Szlapa.
Other titles: World War II survivor's brave story
Description: North Mankato, Minnesota : Capstone Press, [2020] | Series: Graphic library.
   Amazing World War II stories | Includes bibliographical references and index. | Audience:
   Grades 4–6. | Audience: Ages 8–14.
Identifiers: LCCN 2019005963 (print) | LCCN 2019006517 (ebook) | ISBN 9781543573176
   (eBook PDF) | ISBN 9781543573138 (library binding) | ISBN 9781543575484 (paperback)
Subjects: LCSH: Zamperini, Louis, 1917–2014. | Bomber pilots—United States—Biography—
   Juvenile literature. | World War II, 1939–1945—Aerial operations, American—Juvenile
   literature. | Survival—Juvenile literature. | World War II, 1939–1945—Prisoners and prisons,
   Japanese—Juvenile literature. | Prisoners of war—Japan—Biography—Juvenile literature. |
   Prisoners of war—United States—Biography—Juvenile literature.
Classification: LCC D811 (ebook) | LCC D811 .Y565 2020 (print) |
   DDC 940.54/7252092 [B]—dc23
LC record available at https://lccn.loc.gov/2019005963

Summary: In graphic novel format, tells the amazing survival story of Louis Zamperini as he
endures torment and torture as a prisoner of war during World War II.

EDITOR
Aaron J. Sautter

ART DIRECTOR
Nathan Gassman

DESIGNER
Ted Williams

PRODUCTION SPECIALIST
Katy LaVigne

Design Elements by Shutterstock/Guenter Albers

All internet sites appearing in back matter were available and accurate when this book was sent
to press.

Direct quotations appear in **bold italicized text** on the following pages:
Pages 6, 7, 8, 9, 26 : from *Devil at My Heels*, by Louis Zamperini with David Rensin. New York:
   HarperCollins Publishers, 2003.
Pages 11, 15, 19: from *Unbroken: An Olympian's Journey from Airman to Castaway to Captive*,
   by Laura Hilldebrand. New York: Penguin Random House, 2014.

Printed and bound in the United states of America.
122019   000112

TABLE OF CONTENTS

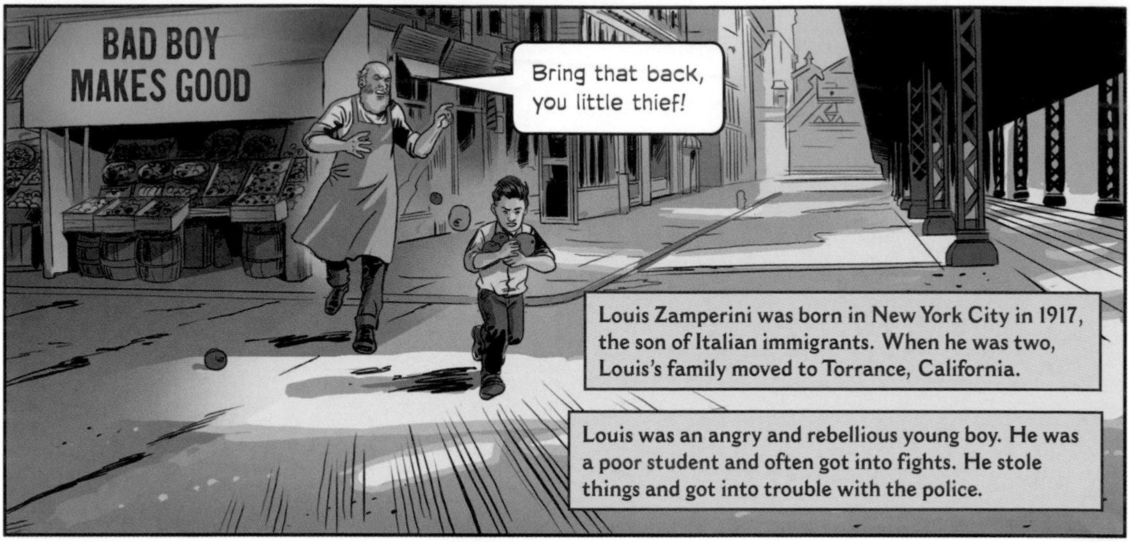
BAD BOY
MAKES GOOD
Bring that back, you little thief!
Louis Zamperini was born in New York City in 1917, the son of Italian immigrants. When he was two, Louis's family moved to Torrance, California.
Louis was an angry and rebellious young boy. He was a poor student and often got into fights. He stole things and got into trouble with the police.

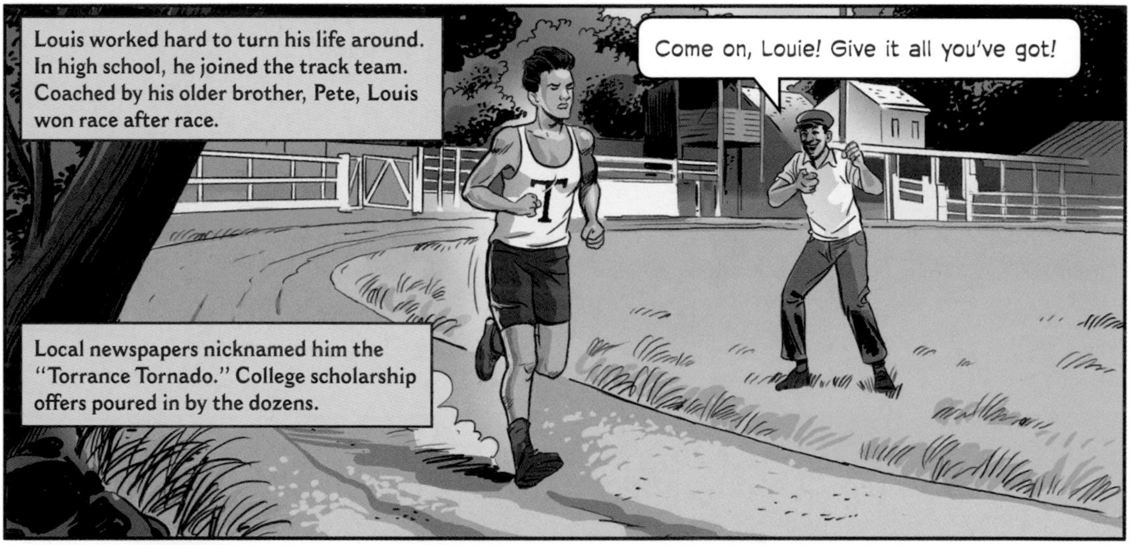
Louis worked hard to turn his life around. In high school, he joined the track team. Coached by his older brother, Pete, Louis won race after race.
Come on, Louie! Give it all you've got!
Local newspapers nicknamed him the "Torrance Tornado." College scholarship offers poured in by the dozens.

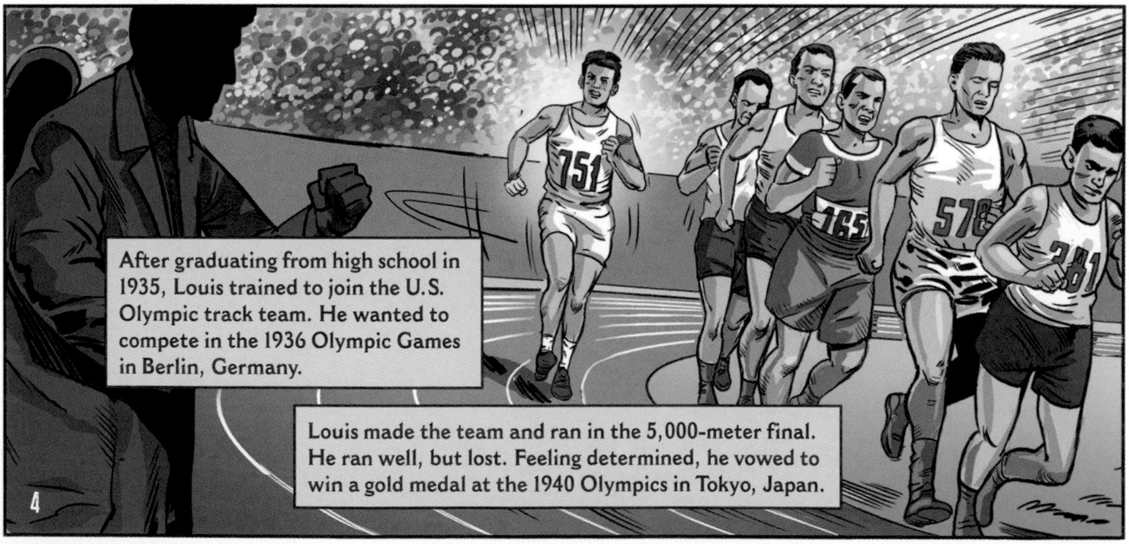
After graduating from high school in 1935, Louis trained to join the U.S. Olympic track team. He wanted to compete in the 1936 Olympic Games in Berlin, Germany.
Louis made the team and ran in the 5,000-meter final. He ran well, but lost. Feeling determined, he vowed to win a gold medal at the 1940 Olympics in Tokyo, Japan.

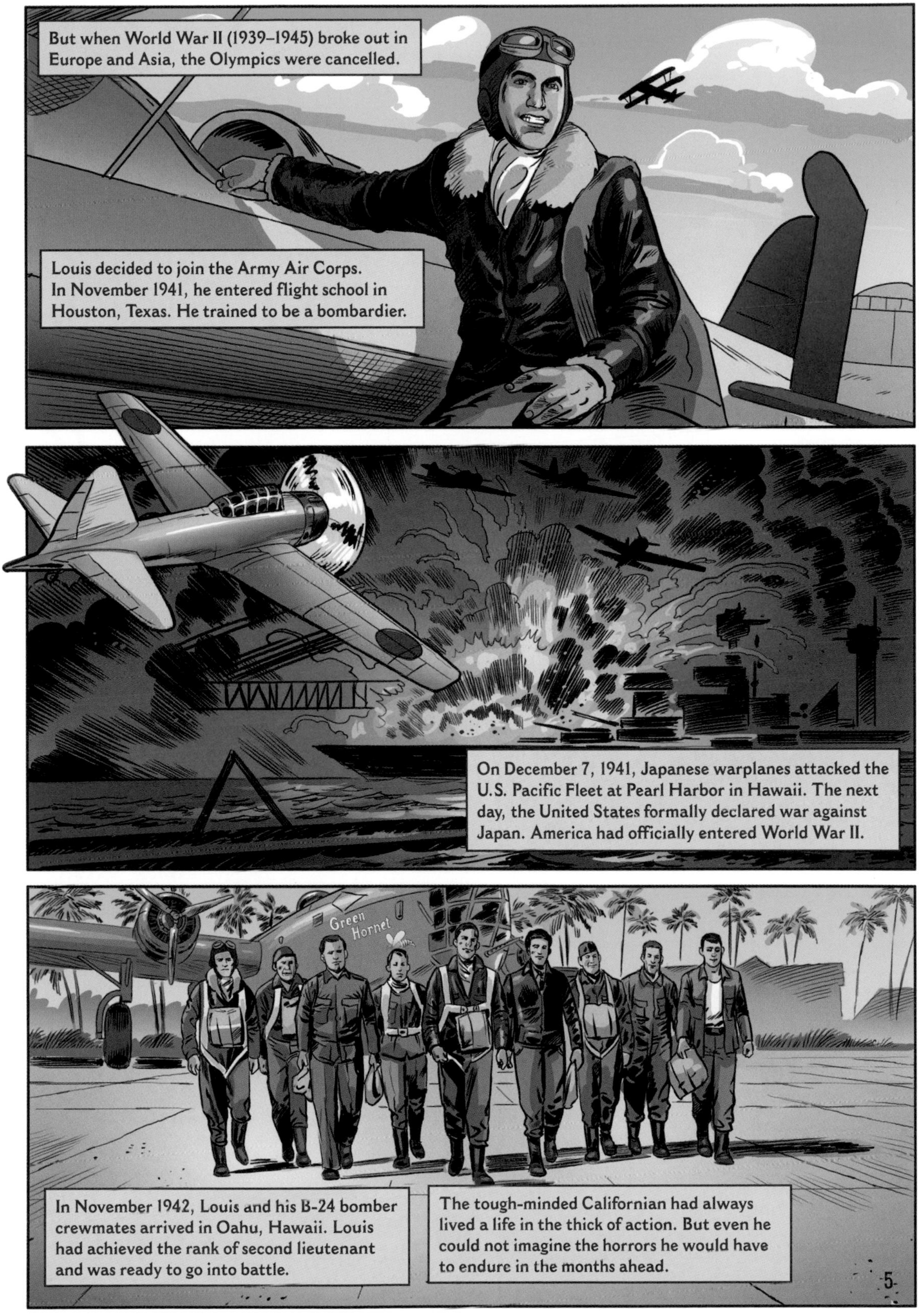

But when World War II (1939–1945) broke out in Europe and Asia, the Olympics were cancelled.
Louis decided to join the Army Air Corps. In November 1941, he entered flight school in Houston, Texas. He trained to be a bombardier.
On December 7, 1941, Japanese warplanes attacked the U.S. Pacific Fleet at Pearl Harbor in Hawaii. The next day, the United States formally declared war against Japan. America had officially entered World War II.
Green Hornet
In November 1942, Louis and his B-24 bomber crewmates arrived in Oahu, Hawaii. Louis had achieved the rank of second lieutenant and was ready to go into battle.
The tough-minded Californian had always lived a life in the thick of action. But even he could not imagine the horrors he would have to endure in the months ahead.

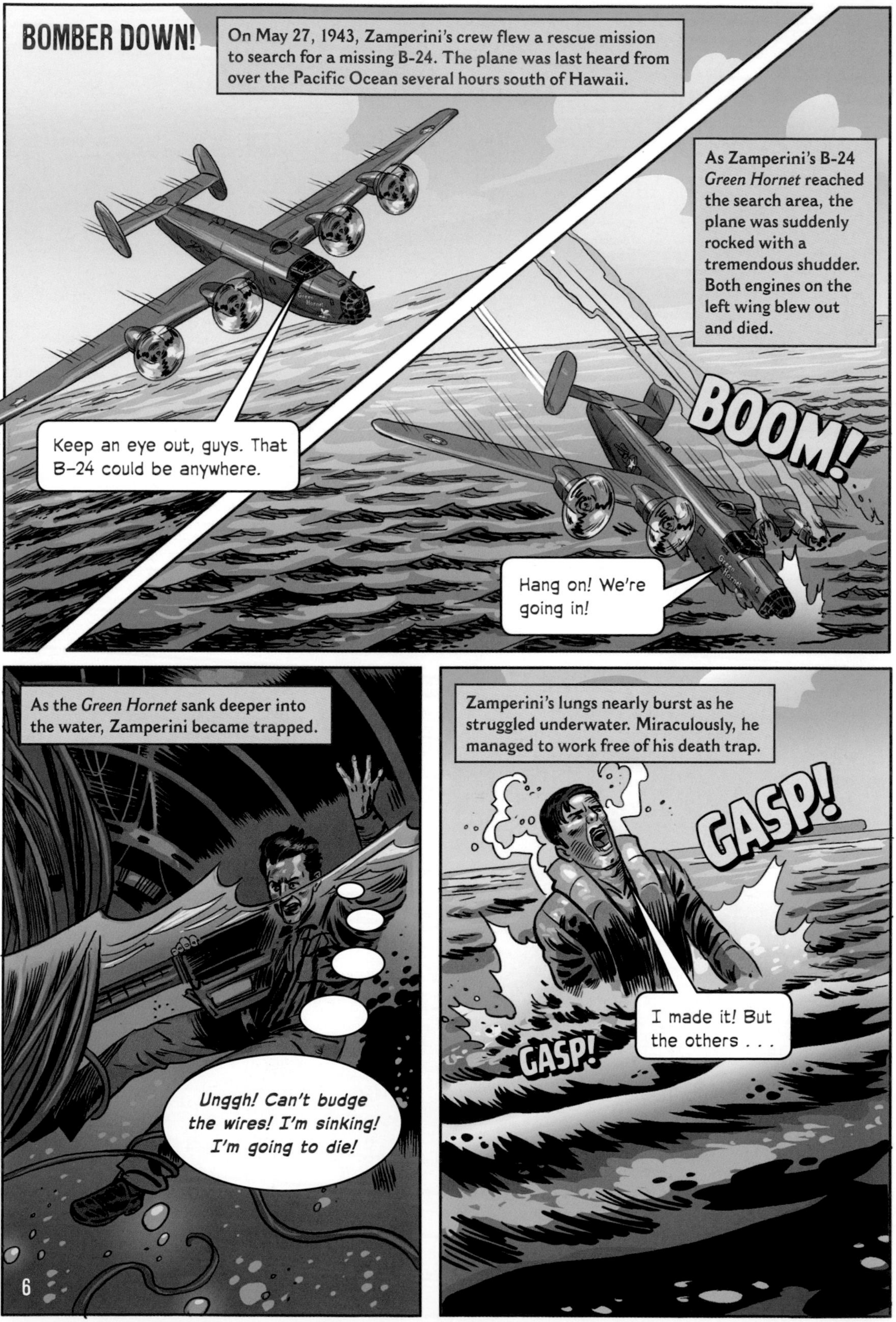
BOMBER DOWN!
On May 27, 1943, Zamperini's crew flew a rescue mission to search for a missing B-24. The plane was last heard from over the Pacific Ocean several hours south of Hawaii.
Keep an eye out, guys. That B-24 could be anywhere.
As Zamperini's B-24 *Green Hornet* reached the search area, the plane was suddenly rocked with a tremendous shudder. Both engines on the left wing blew out and died.
BOOM!
Hang on! We're going in!
As the *Green Hornet* sank deeper into the water, Zamperini became trapped.
Unggh! Can't budge the wires! I'm sinking! I'm going to die!
Zamperini's lungs nearly burst as he struggled underwater. Miraculously, he managed to work free of his death trap.
GASP!
GASP!
I made it! But the others . . .

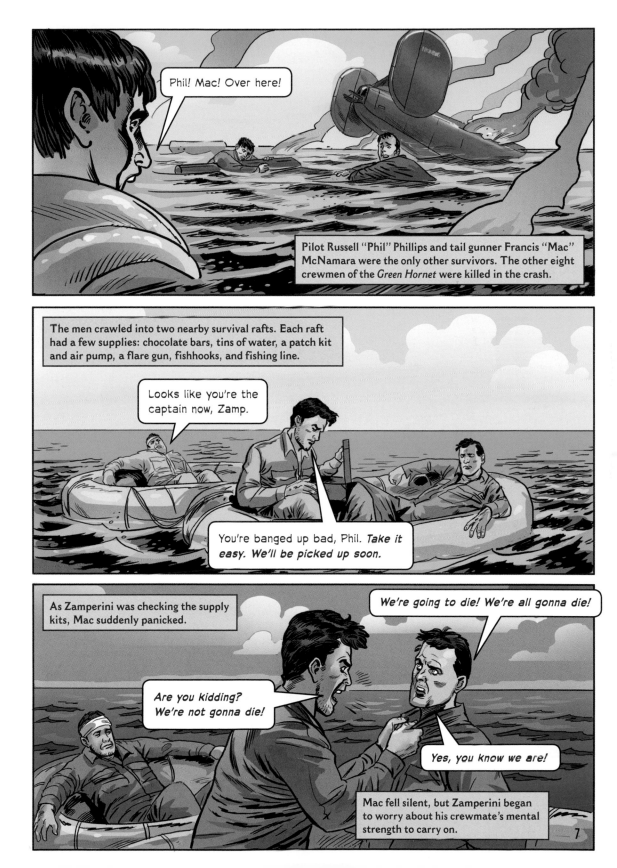

Phil! Mac! Over here!

Pilot Russell "Phil" Phillips and tail gunner Francis "Mac" McNamara were the only other survivors. The other eight crewmen of the *Green Hornet* were killed in the crash.

The men crawled into two nearby survival rafts. Each raft had a few supplies: chocolate bars, tins of water, a patch kit and air pump, a flare gun, fishhooks, and fishing line.

Looks like you're the captain now, Zamp.

You're banged up bad, Phil. *Take it easy. We'll be picked up soon.*

As Zamperini was checking the supply kits, Mac suddenly panicked.

We're going to die! We're all gonna die!

Are you kidding? We're not gonna die!

Yes, you know we are!

Mac fell silent, but Zamperini began to worry about his crewmate's mental strength to carry on.

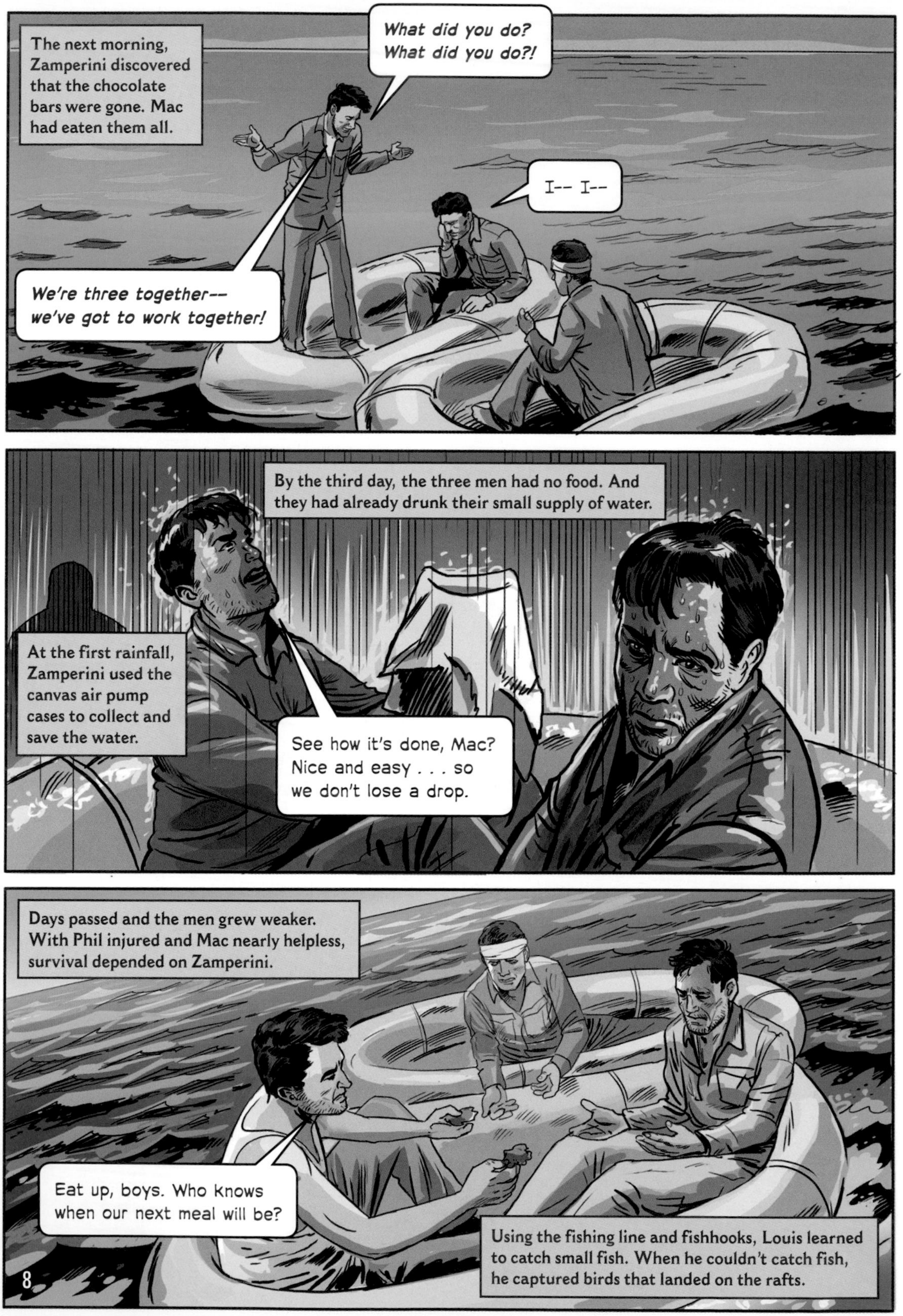
The next morning, Zamperini discovered that the chocolate bars were gone. Mac had eaten them all.
What did you do? What did you do?!
We're three together-- we've got to work together!
I-- I--
By the third day, the three men had no food. And they had already drunk their small supply of water.
At the first rainfall, Zamperini used the canvas air pump cases to collect and save the water.
See how it's done, Mac? Nice and easy . . . so we don't lose a drop.
Days passed and the men grew weaker. With Phil injured and Mac nearly helpless, survival depended on Zamperini.
Eat up, boys. Who knows when our next meal will be?
Using the fishing line and fishhooks, Louis learned to catch small fish. When he couldn't catch fish, he captured birds that landed on the rafts.

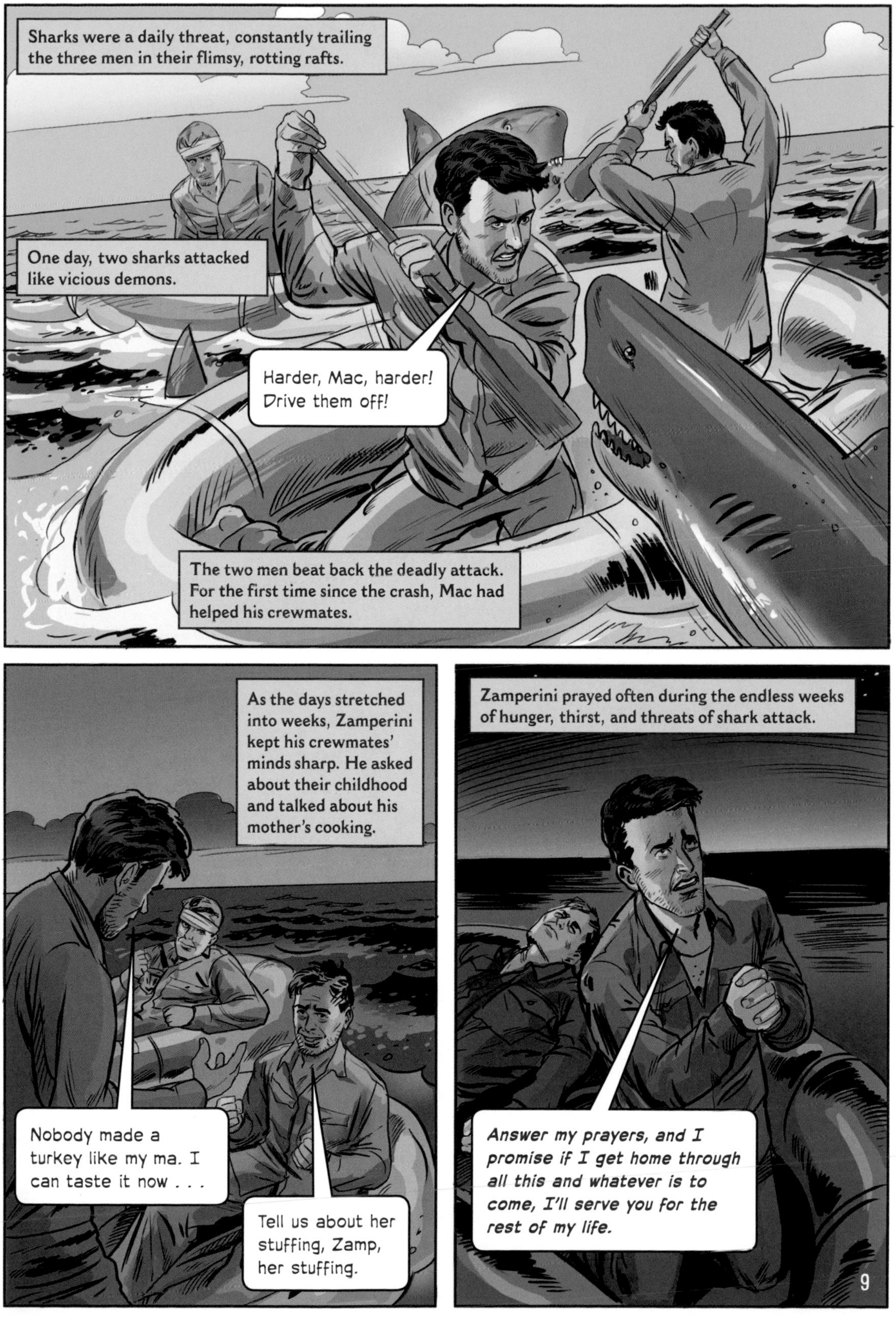
Sharks were a daily threat, constantly trailing the three men in their flimsy, rotting rafts.
One day, two sharks attacked like vicious demons.
Harder, Mac, harder! Drive them off!
The two men beat back the deadly attack. For the first time since the crash, Mac had helped his crewmates.
As the days stretched into weeks, Zamperini kept his crewmates' minds sharp. He asked about their childhood and talked about his mother's cooking.
Nobody made a turkey like my ma. I can taste it now . . .
Tell us about her stuffing, Zamp, her stuffing.
Zamperini prayed often during the endless weeks of hunger, thirst, and threats of shark attack.
Answer my prayers, and I promise if I get home through all this and whatever is to come, I'll serve you for the rest of my life.

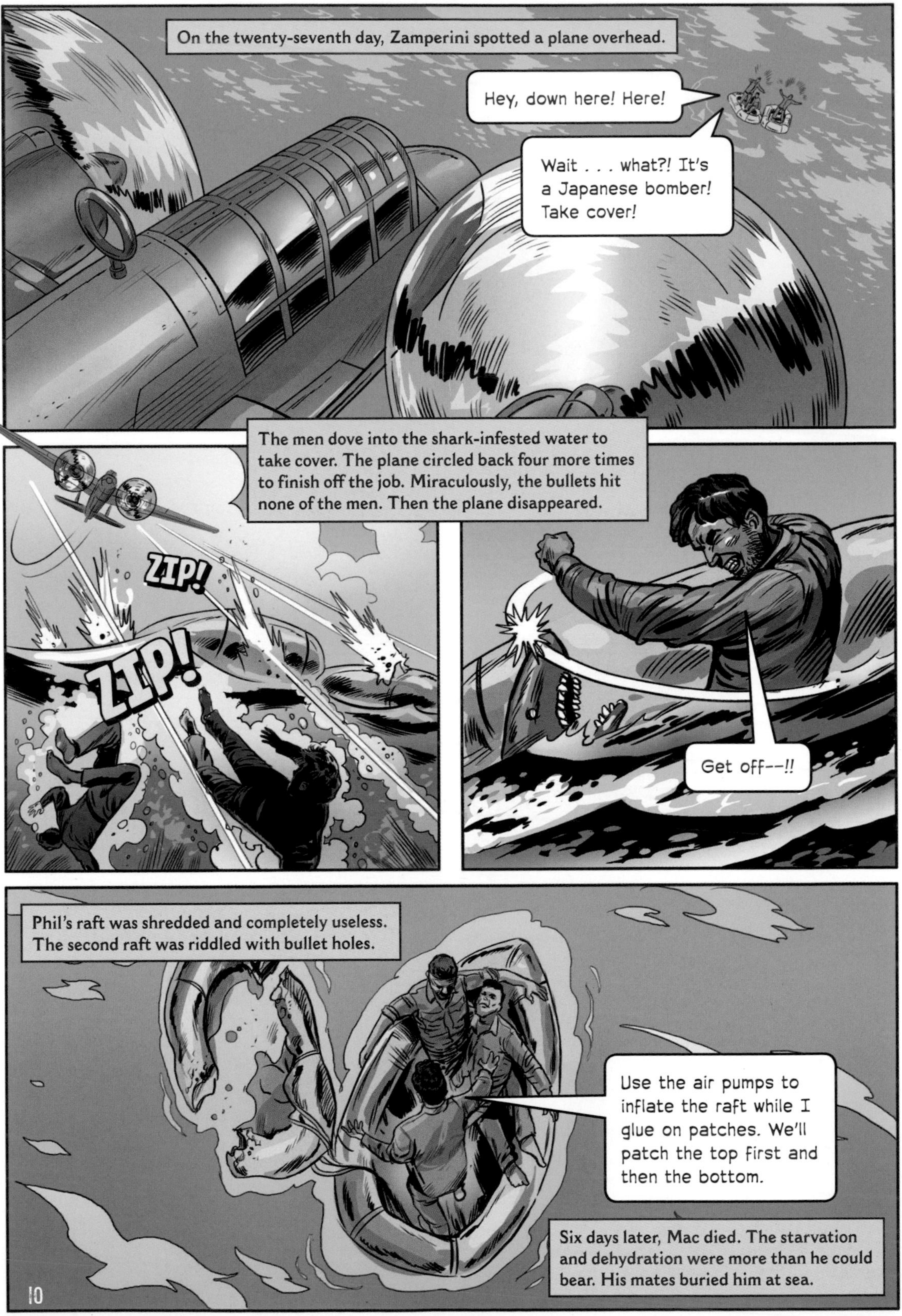
On the twenty-seventh day, Zamperini spotted a plane overhead.
Hey, down here! Here!
Wait . . . what?! It's a Japanese bomber! Take cover!
The men dove into the shark-infested water to take cover. The plane circled back four more times to finish off the job. Miraculously, the bullets hit none of the men. Then the plane disappeared.
ZIP!
ZIP!
Get off--!!
Phil's raft was shredded and completely useless. The second raft was riddled with bullet holes.
Use the air pumps to inflate the raft while I glue on patches. We'll patch the top first and then the bottom.
Six days later, Mac died. The starvation and dehydration were more than he could bear. His mates buried him at sea.

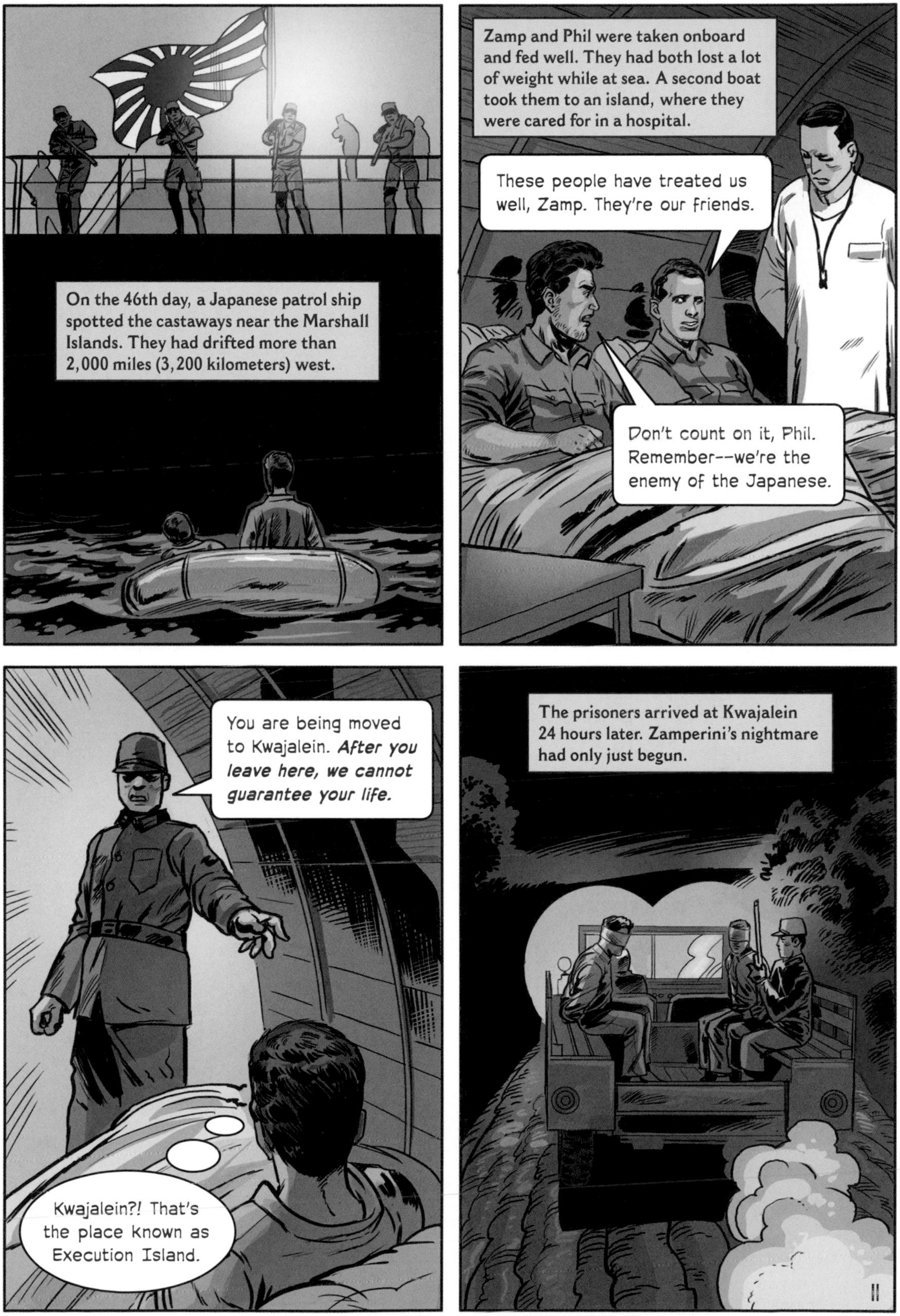
On the 46th day, a Japanese patrol ship spotted the castaways near the Marshall Islands. They had drifted more than 2,000 miles (3,200 kilometers) west.
Zamp and Phil were taken onboard and fed well. They had both lost a lot of weight while at sea. A second boat took them to an island, where they were cared for in a hospital.
These people have treated us well, Zamp. They're our friends.
Don't count on it, Phil. Remember--we're the enemy of the Japanese.
You are being moved to Kwajalein. *After you leave here, we cannot guarantee your life.*
Kwajalein?! That's the place known as Execution Island.
The prisoners arrived at Kwajalein 24 hours later. Zamperini's nightmare had only just begun.

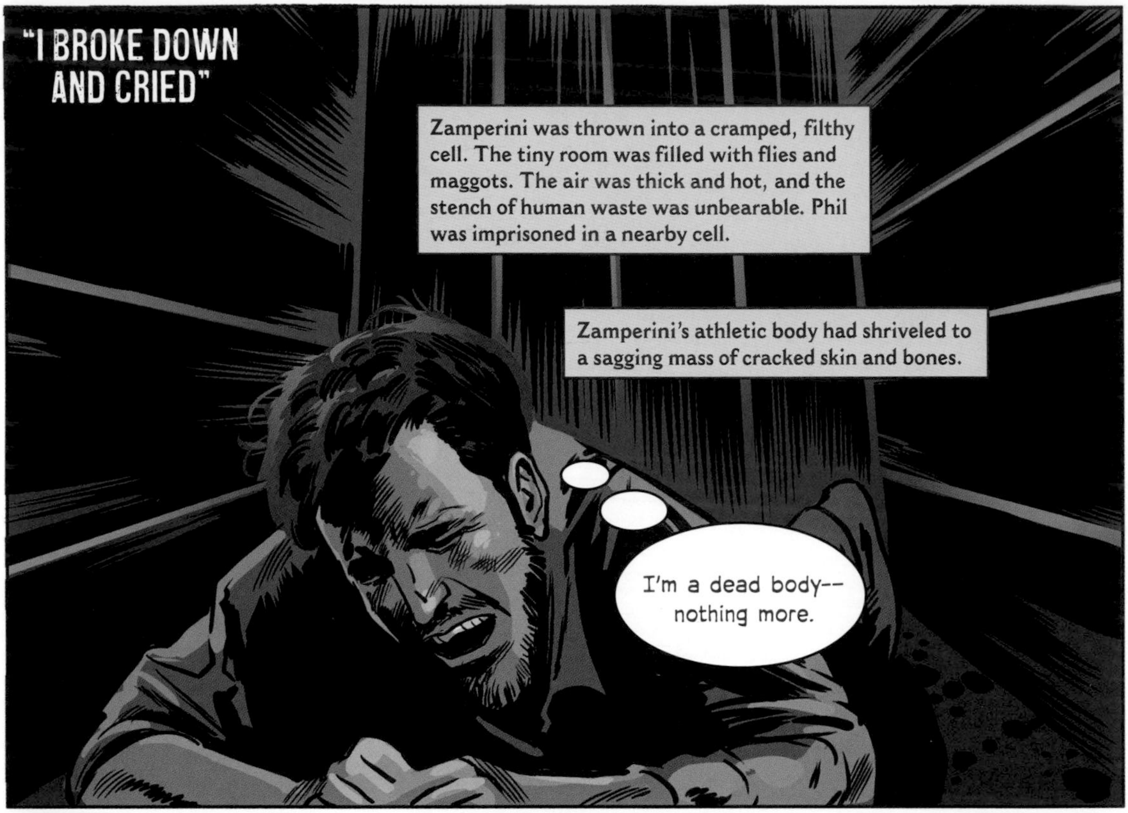
"I BROKE DOWN AND CRIED"
Zamperini was thrown into a cramped, filthy cell. The tiny room was filled with flies and maggots. The air was thick and hot, and the stench of human waste was unbearable. Phil was imprisoned in a nearby cell.
Zamperini's athletic body had shriveled to a sagging mass of cracked skin and bones.
I'm a dead body-- nothing more.

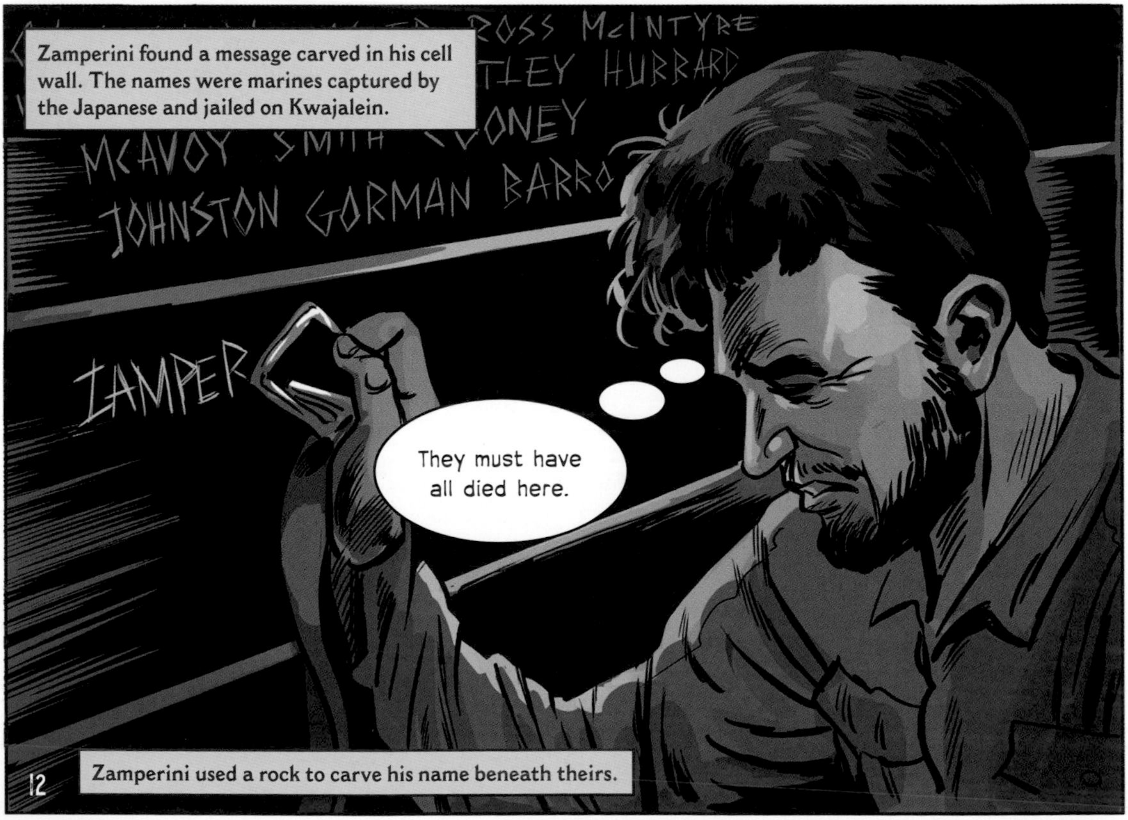
Zamperini found a message carved in his cell wall. The names were marines captured by the Japanese and jailed on Kwajalein.
McINTYRE
SMITH
JOHNSTON GORMAN
They must have all died here.
Zamperini used a rock to carve his name beneath theirs.

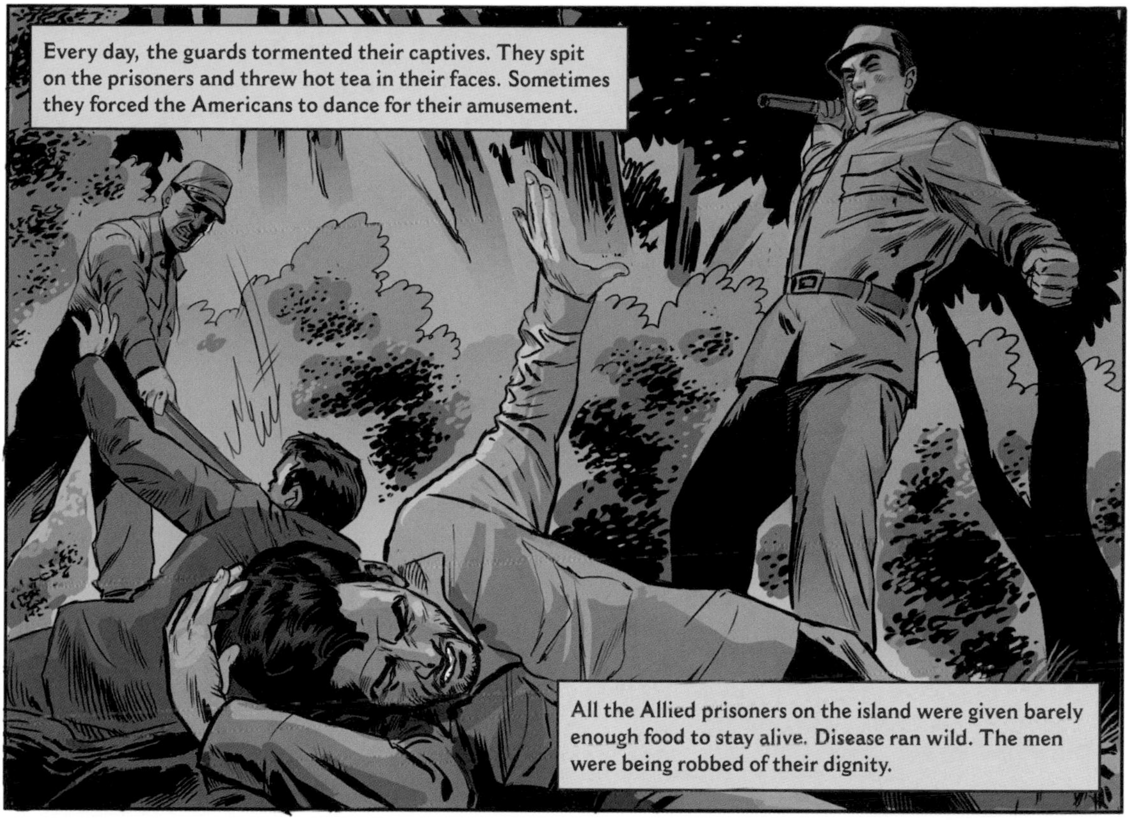
Every day, the guards tormented their captives. They spit on the prisoners and threw hot tea in their faces. Sometimes they forced the Americans to dance for their amusement.
All the Allied prisoners on the island were given barely enough food to stay alive. Disease ran wild. The men were being robbed of their dignity.

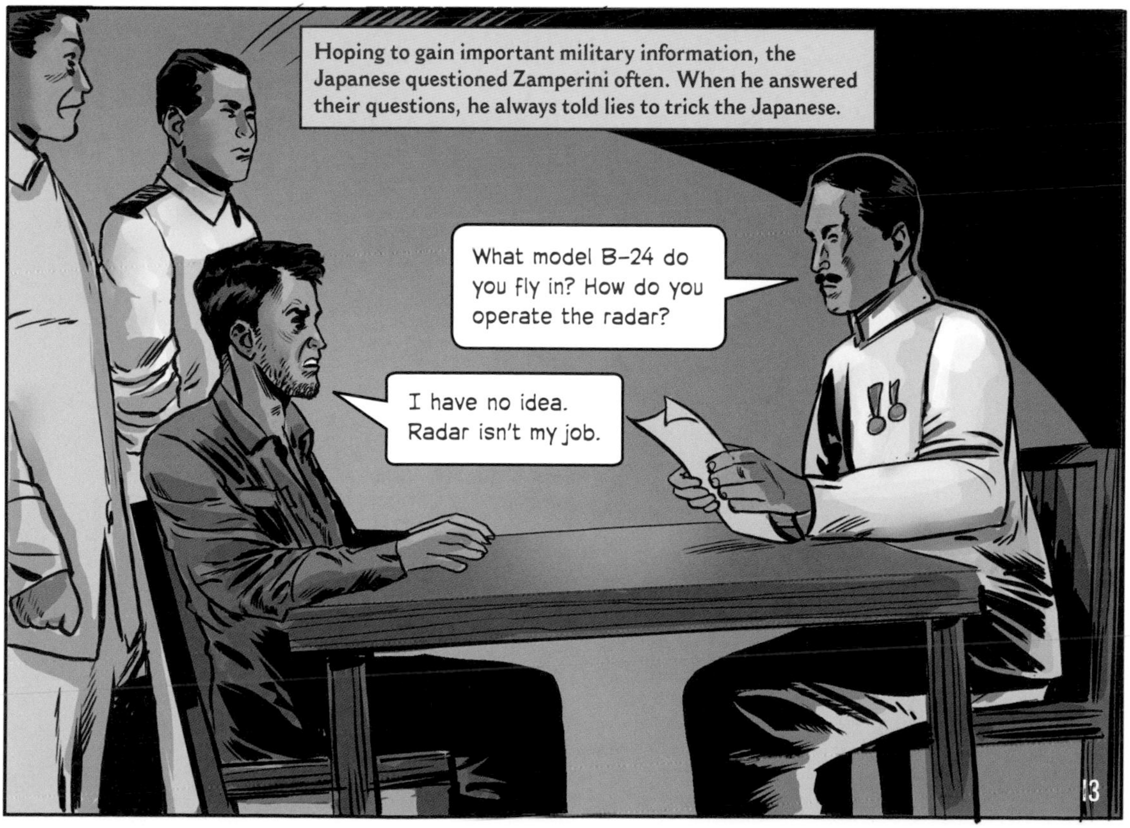
Hoping to gain important military information, the Japanese questioned Zamperini often. When he answered their questions, he always told lies to trick the Japanese.
What model B-24 do you fly in? How do you operate the radar?
I have no idea. Radar isn't my job.

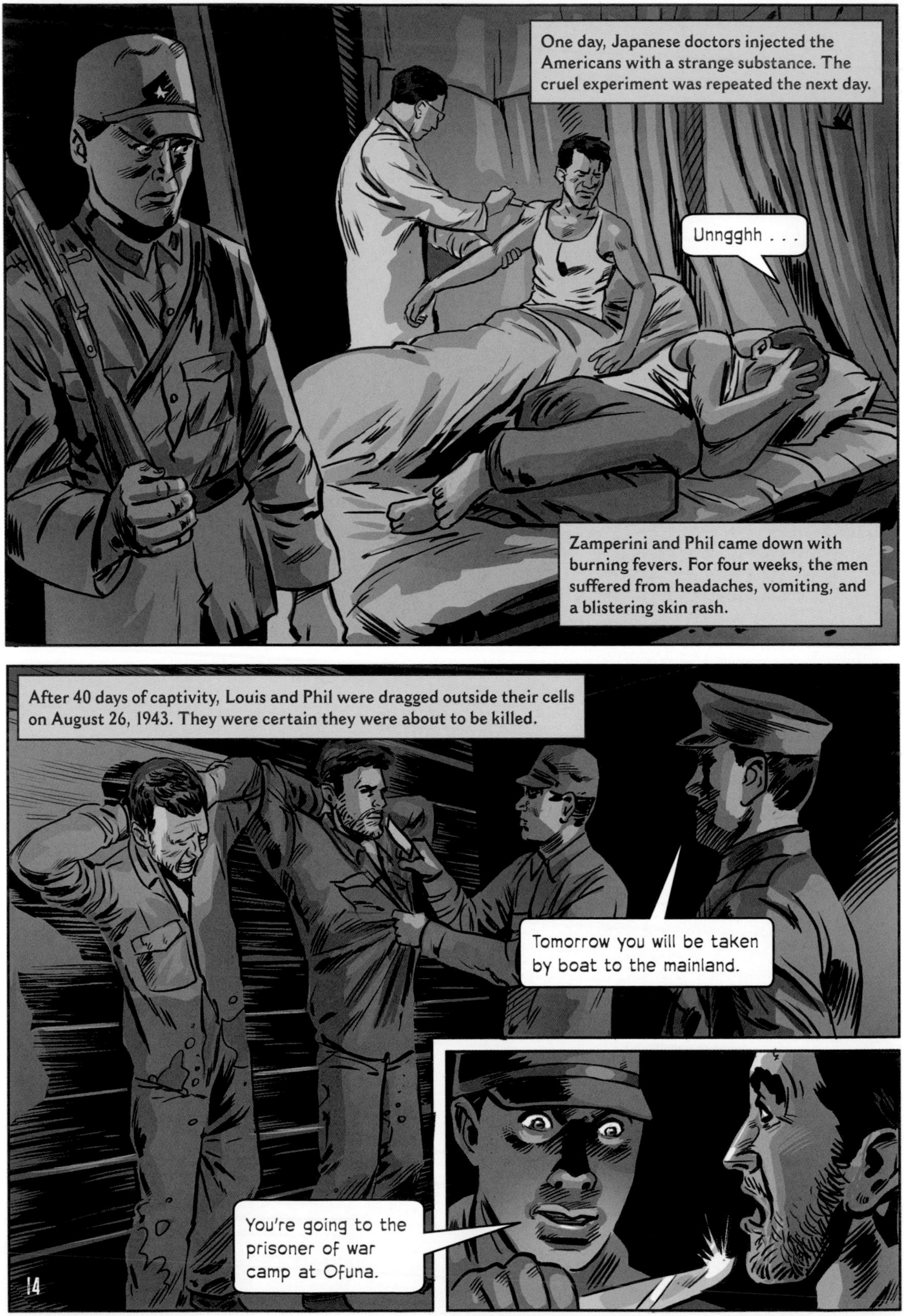
One day, Japanese doctors injected the Americans with a strange substance. The cruel experiment was repeated the next day.
Unngghh . . .
Zamperini and Phil came down with burning fevers. For four weeks, the men suffered from headaches, vomiting, and a blistering skin rash.
After 40 days of captivity, Louis and Phil were dragged outside their cells on August 26, 1943. They were certain they were about to be killed.
Tomorrow you will be taken by boat to the mainland.
You're going to the prisoner of war camp at Ofuna.

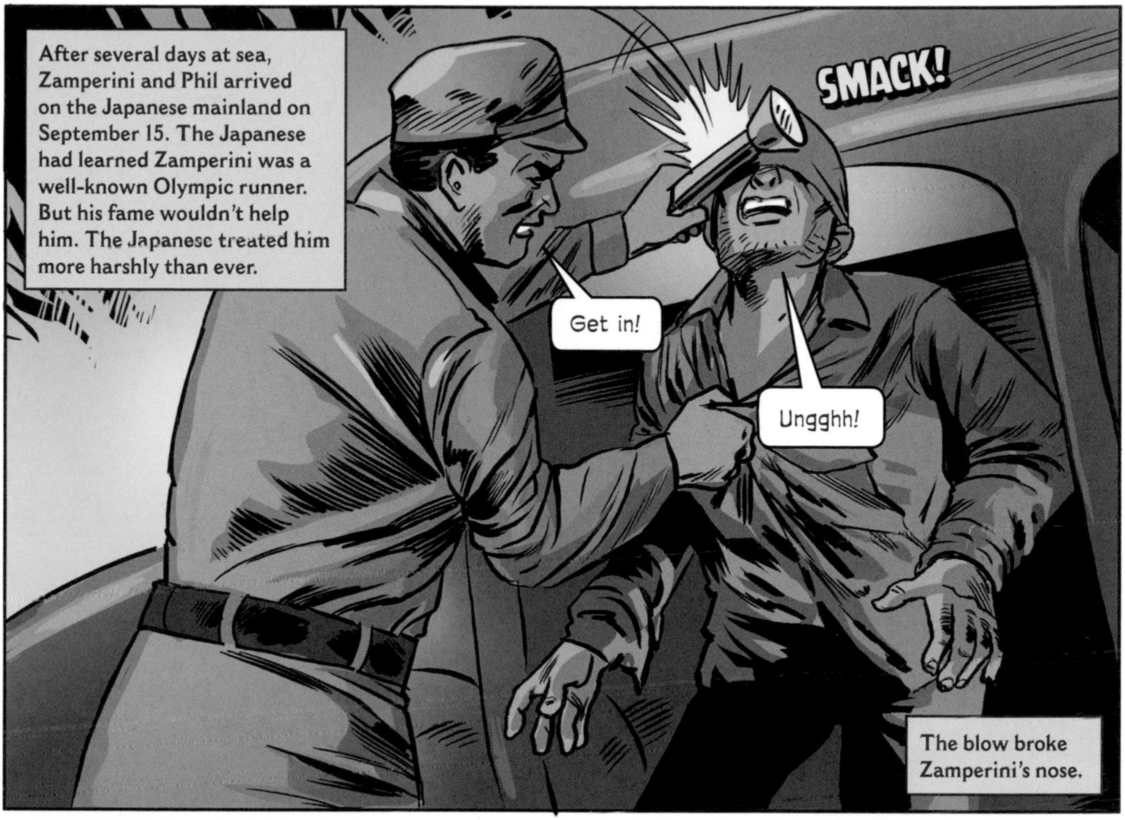
After several days at sea, Zamperini and Phil arrived on the Japanese mainland on September 15. The Japanese had learned Zamperini was a well-known Olympic runner. But his fame wouldn't help him. The Japanese treated him more harshly than ever.
SMACK!
Get in!
Ungghh!
The blow broke Zamperini's nose.

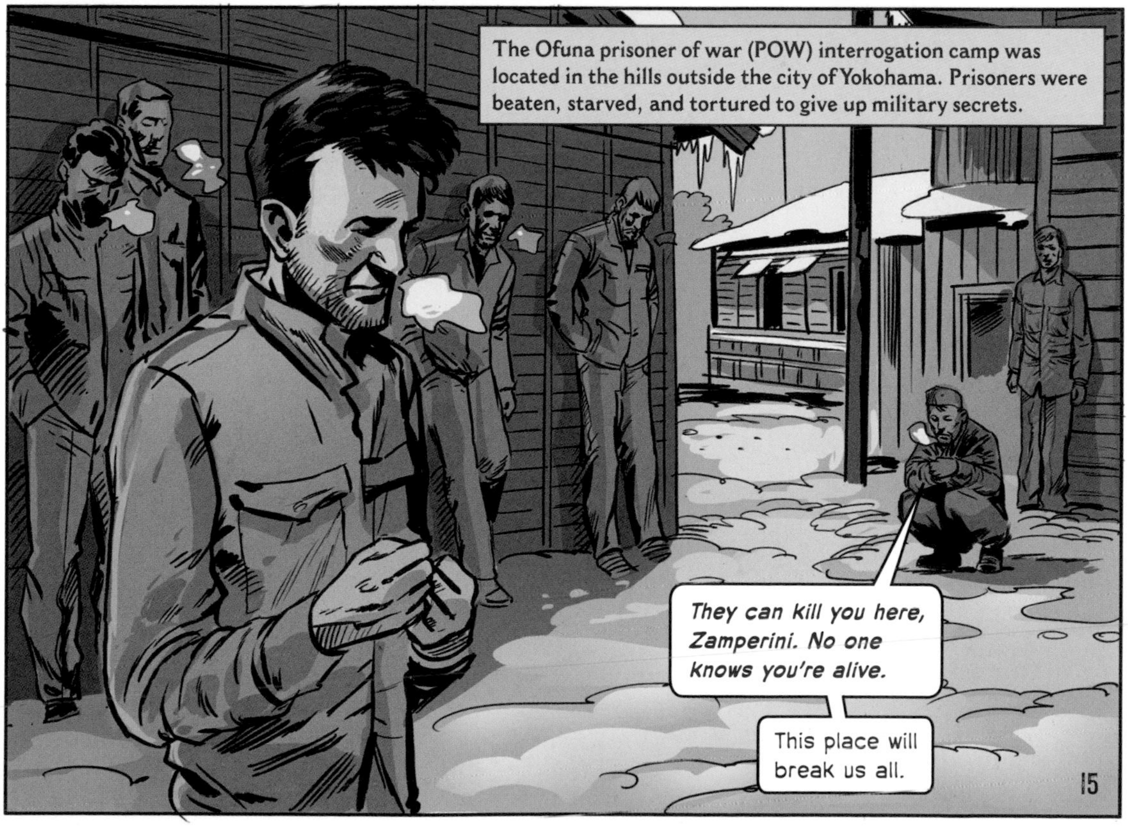
The Ofuna prisoner of war (POW) interrogation camp was located in the hills outside the city of Yokohama. Prisoners were beaten, starved, and tortured to give up military secrets.
They can kill you here, Zamperini. No one knows you're alive.
This place will break us all.

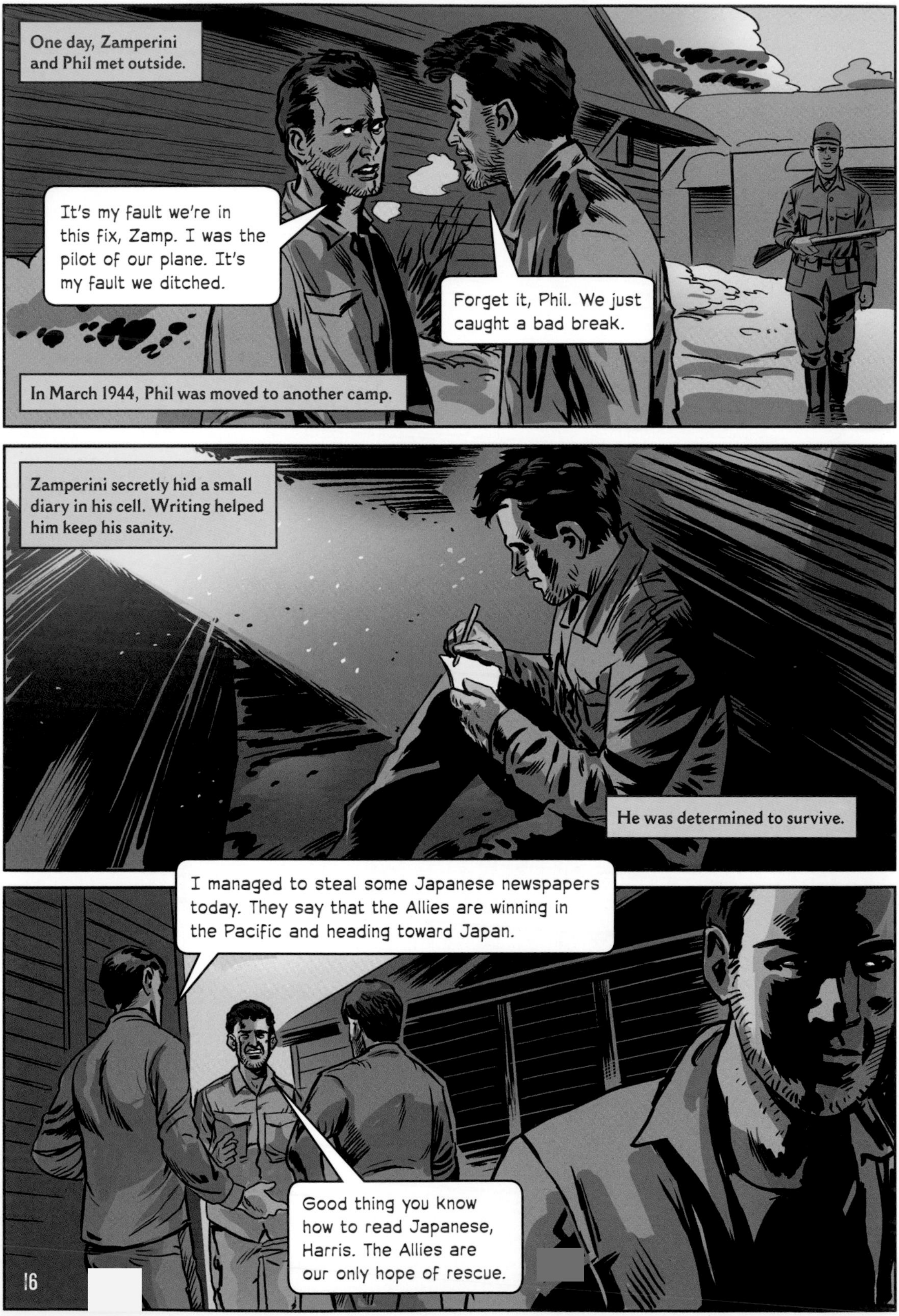
One day, Zamperini and Phil met outside.
It's my fault we're in this fix, Zamp. I was the pilot of our plane. It's my fault we ditched.
Forget it, Phil. We just caught a bad break.
In March 1944, Phil was moved to another camp.
Zamperini secretly hid a small diary in his cell. Writing helped him keep his sanity.
He was determined to survive.
I managed to steal some Japanese newspapers today. They say that the Allies are winning in the Pacific and heading toward Japan.
Good thing you know how to read Japanese, Harris. The Allies are our only hope of rescue.

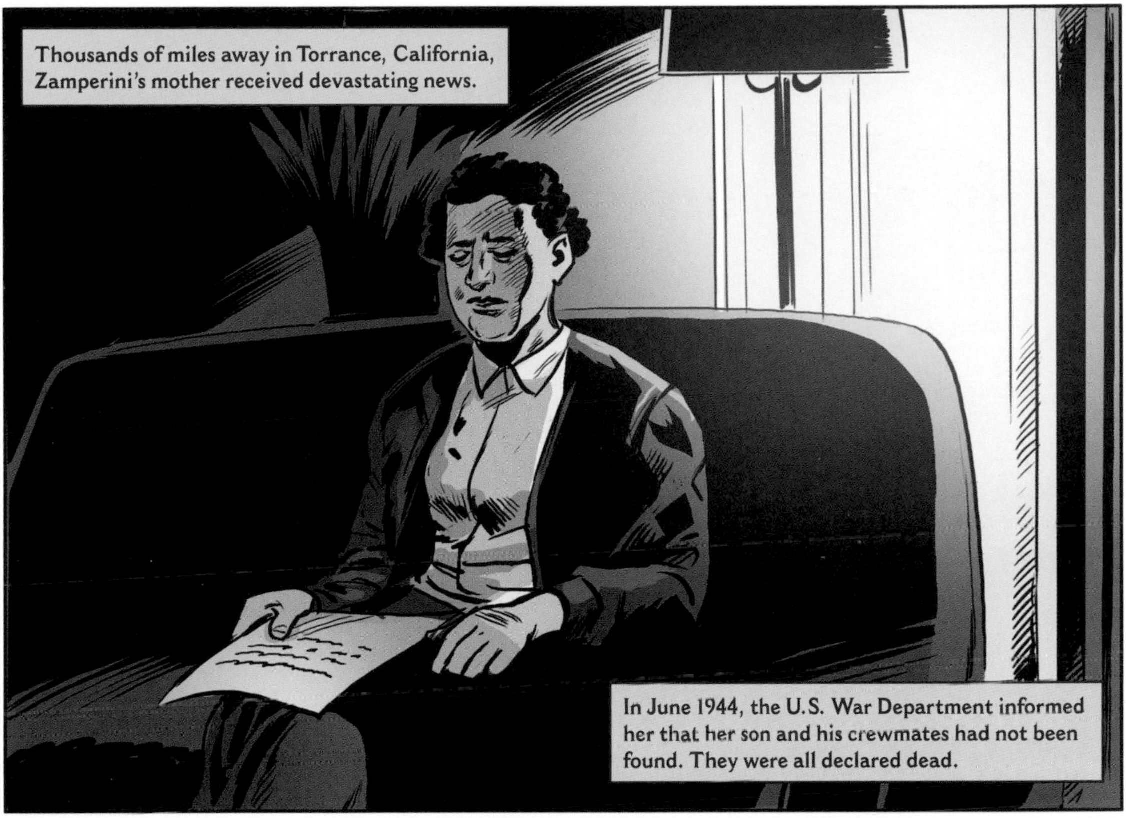
Thousands of miles away in Torrance, California, Zamperini's mother received devastating news.
In June 1944, the U.S. War Department informed her that her son and his crewmates had not been found. They were all declared dead.

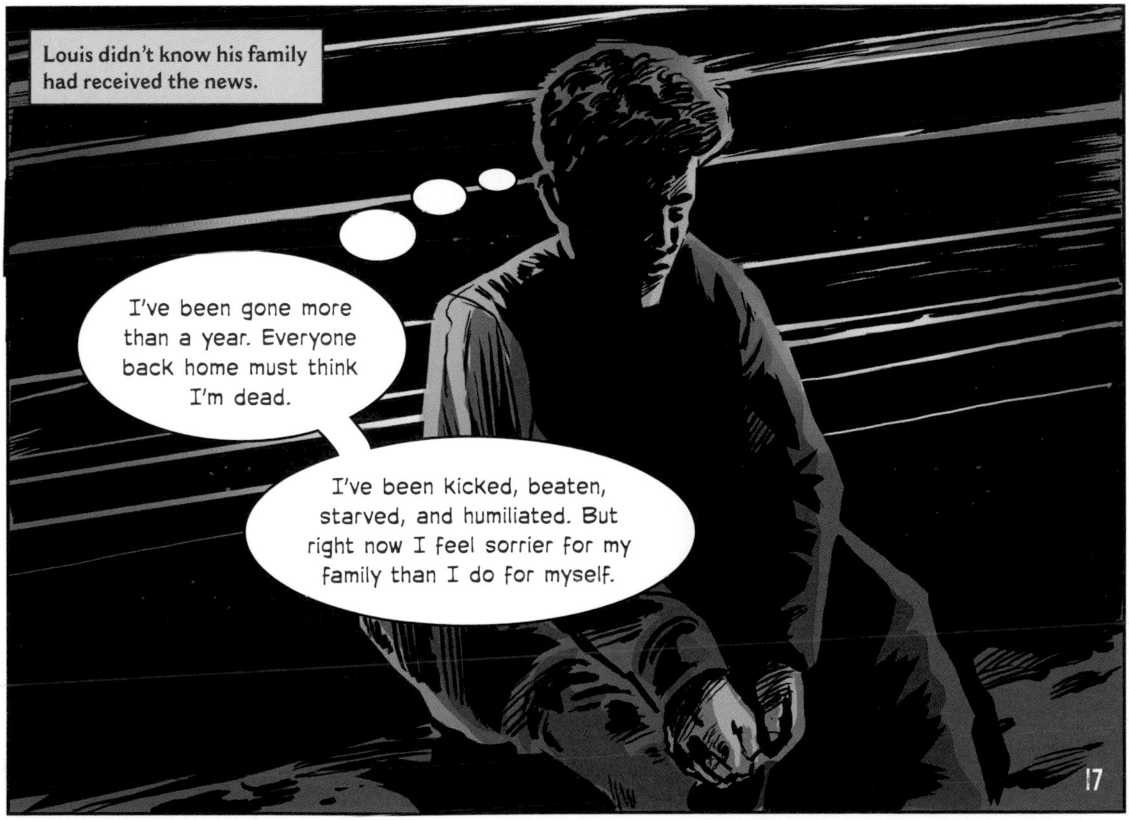
Louis didn't know his family had received the news.
I've been gone more than a year. Everyone back home must think I'm dead.
I've been kicked, beaten, starved, and humiliated. But right now I feel sorrier for my family than I do for myself.

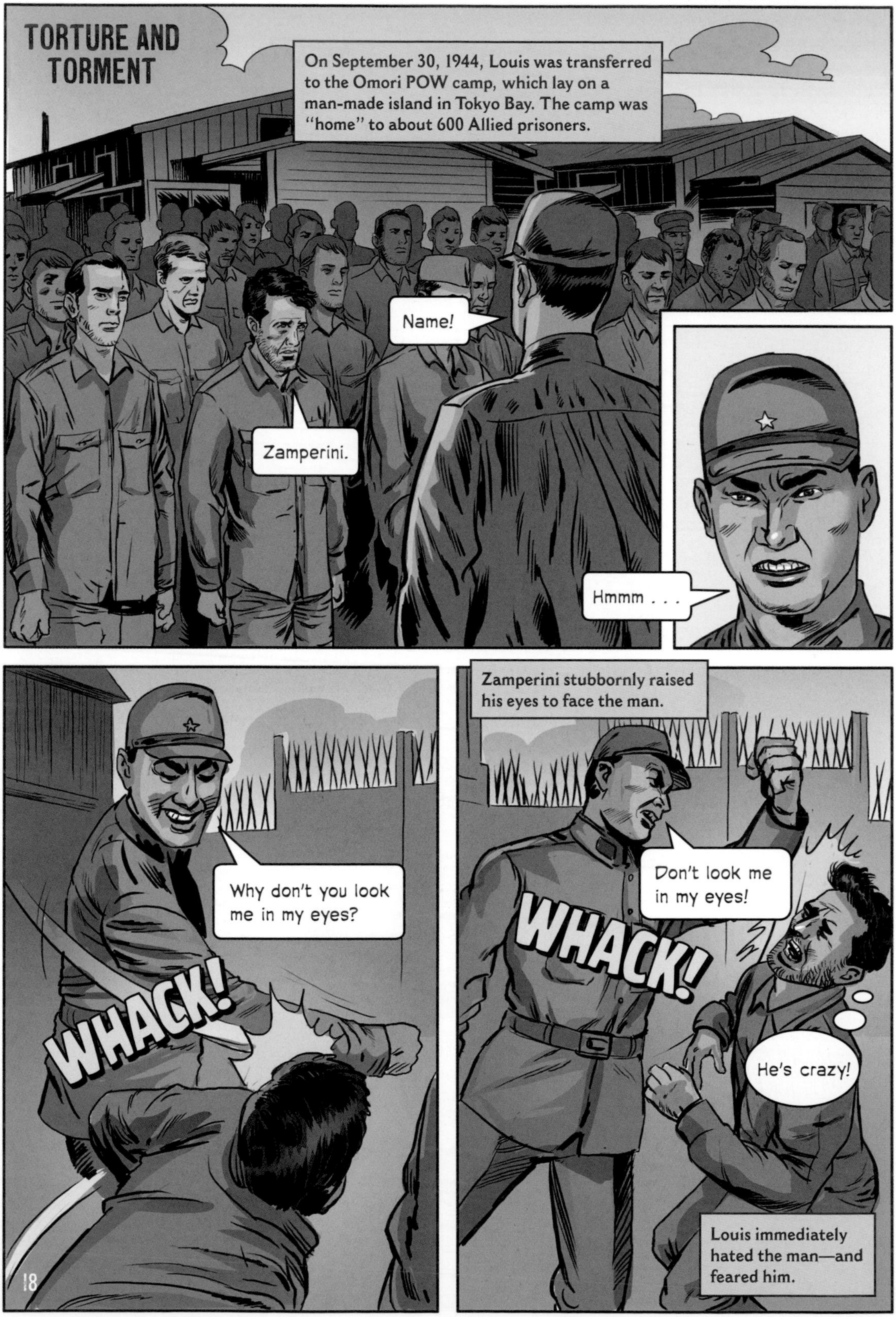
TORTURE AND TORMENT
On September 30, 1944, Louis was transferred to the Omori POW camp, which lay on a man-made island in Tokyo Bay. The camp was "home" to about 600 Allied prisoners.
Name!
Zamperini.
Hmmm . . .
Why don't you look me in my eyes?
WHACK!
Zamperini stubbornly raised his eyes to face the man.
Don't look me in my eyes!
WHACK!
He's crazy!
Louis immediately hated the man—and feared him.

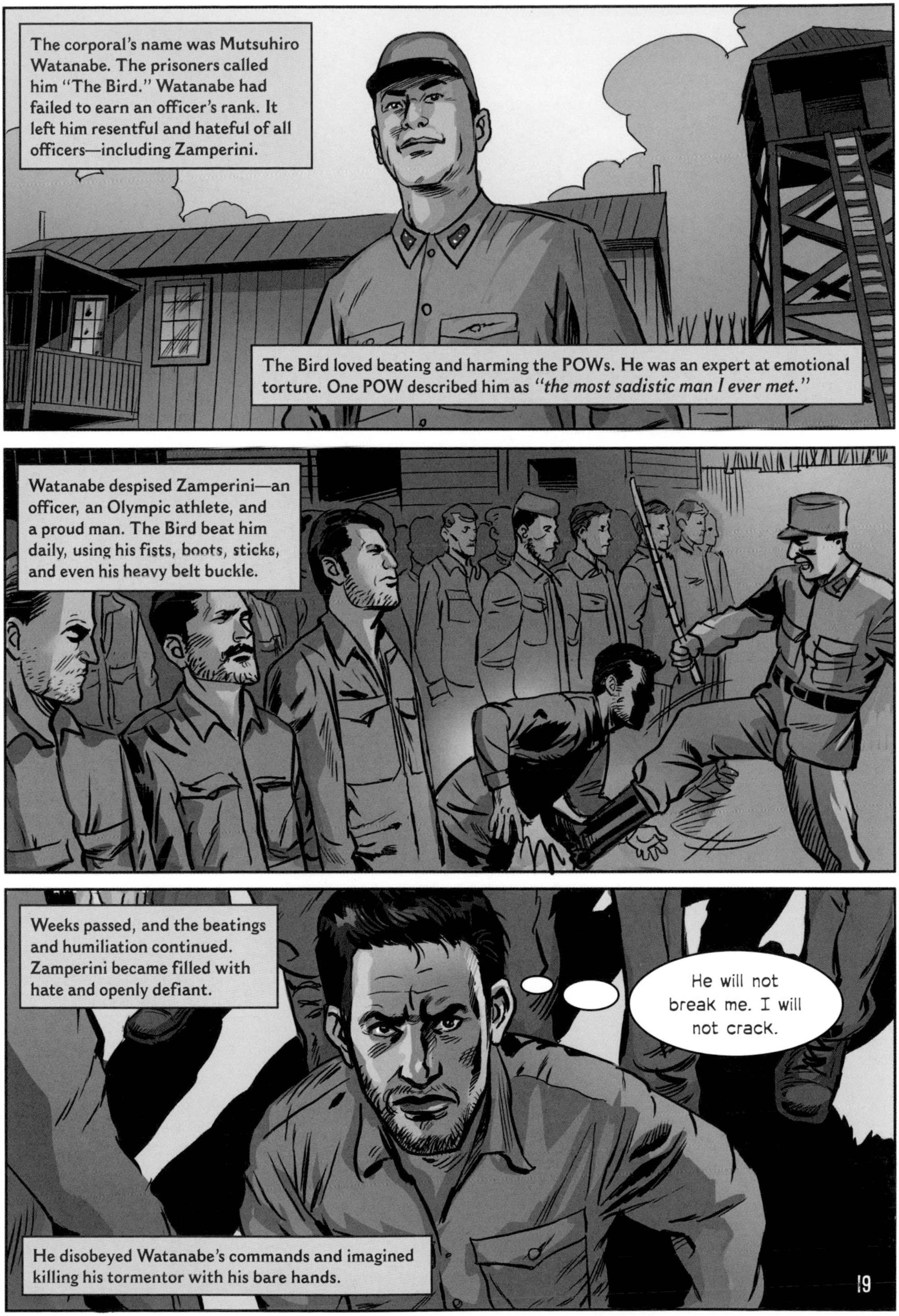
The corporal's name was Mutsuhiro Watanabe. The prisoners called him "The Bird." Watanabe had failed to earn an officer's rank. It left him resentful and hateful of all officers—including Zamperini.
The Bird loved beating and harming the POWs. He was an expert at emotional torture. One POW described him as *"the most sadistic man I ever met."*
Watanabe despised Zamperini—an officer, an Olympic athlete, and a proud man. The Bird beat him daily, using his fists, boots, sticks, and even his heavy belt buckle.
Weeks passed, and the beatings and humiliation continued. Zamperini became filled with hate and openly defiant.
He will not break me. I will not crack.
He disobeyed Watanabe's commands and imagined killing his tormentor with his bare hands.

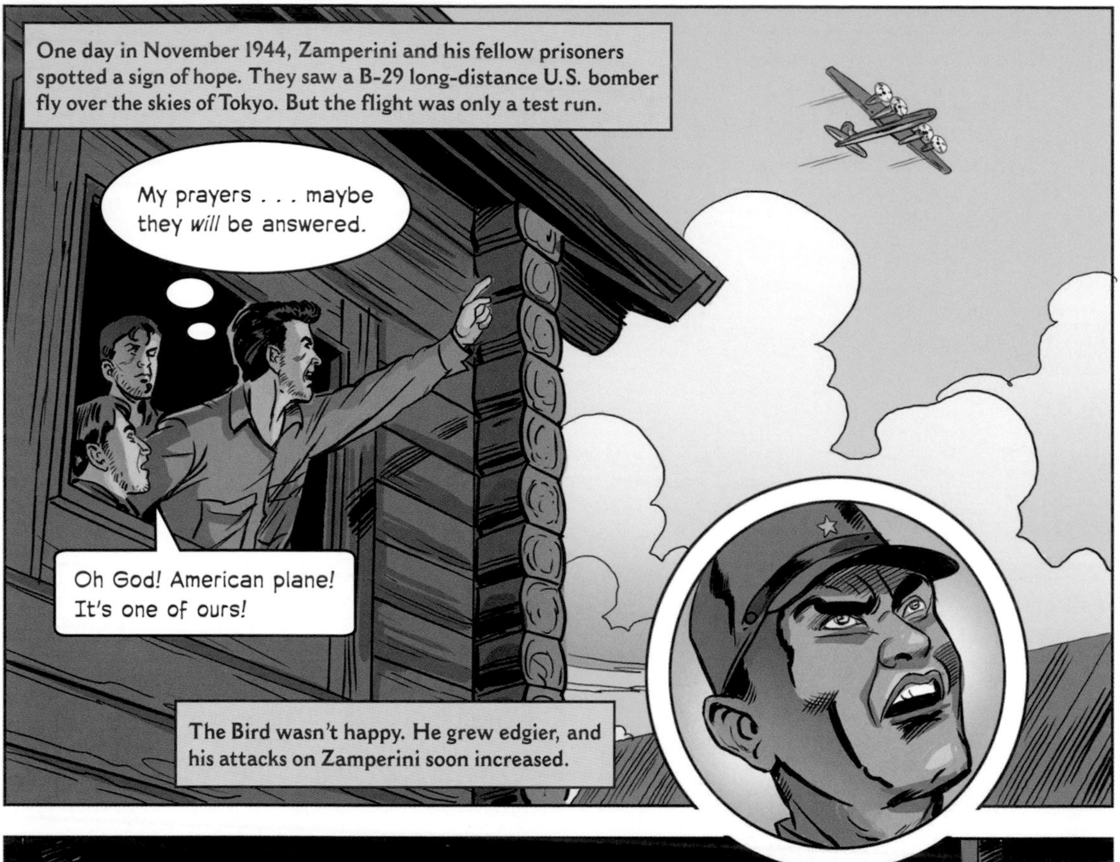
One day in November 1944, Zamperini and his fellow prisoners spotted a sign of hope. They saw a B-29 long-distance U.S. bomber fly over the skies of Tokyo. But the flight was only a test run.
Oh God! American plane! It's one of ours!
My prayers . . . maybe they *will* be answered.
The Bird wasn't happy. He grew edgier, and his attacks on Zamperini soon increased.

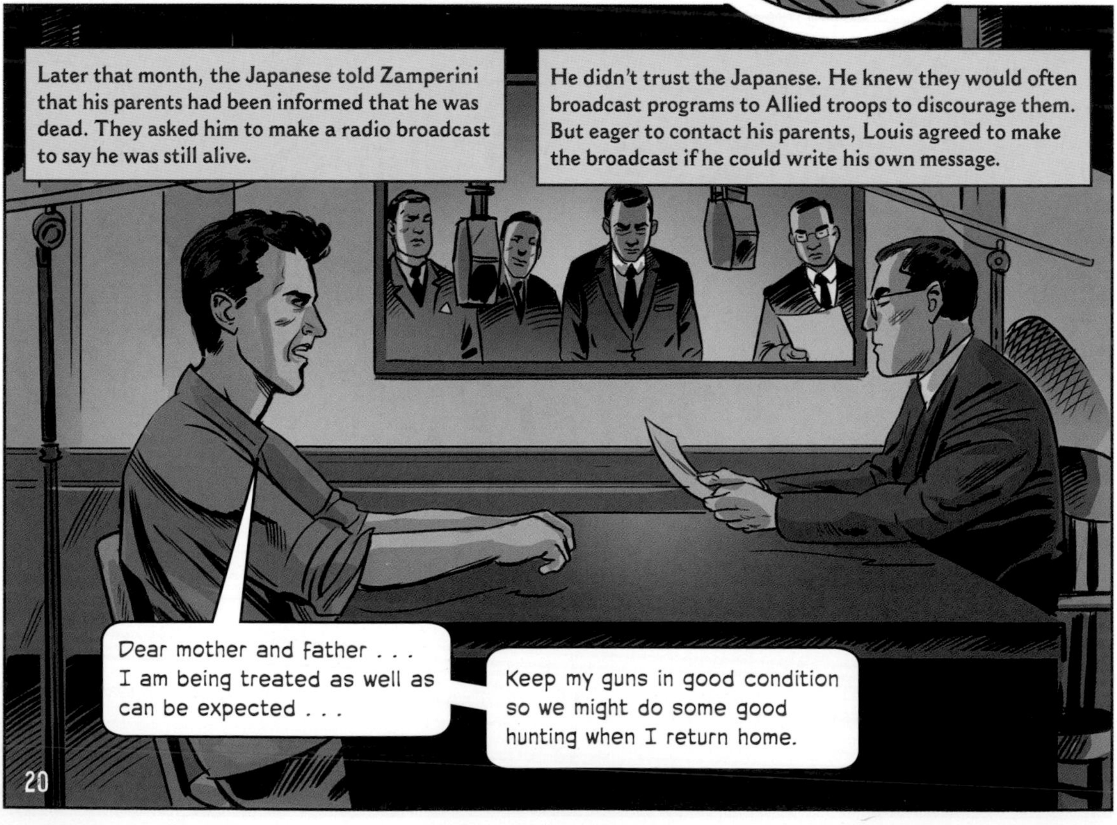
Later that month, the Japanese told Zamperini that his parents had been informed that he was dead. They asked him to make a radio broadcast to say he was still alive.
He didn't trust the Japanese. He knew they would often broadcast programs to Allied troops to discourage them. But eager to contact his parents, Louis agreed to make the broadcast if he could write his own message.
Dear mother and father . . . I am being treated as well as can be expected . . .
Keep my guns in good condition so we might do some good hunting when I return home.

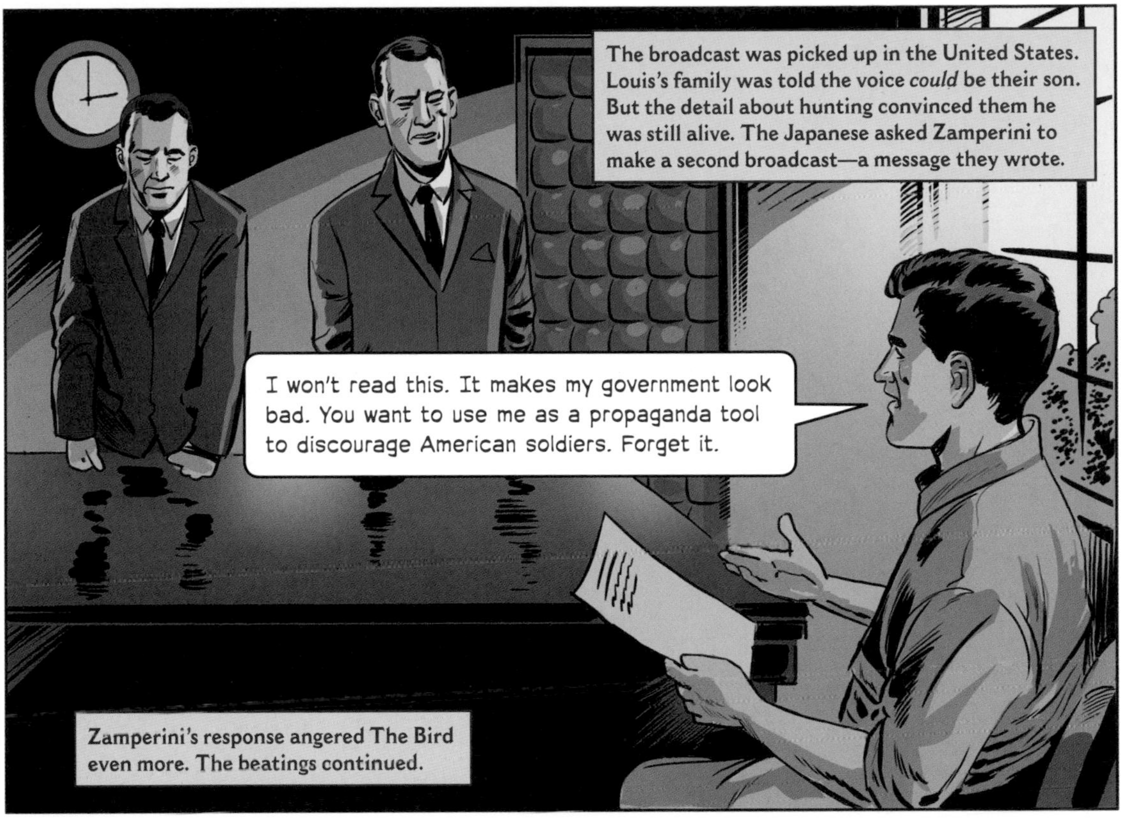
The broadcast was picked up in the United States. Louis's family was told the voice *could* be their son. But the detail about hunting convinced them he was still alive. The Japanese asked Zamperini to make a second broadcast—a message they wrote.
I won't read this. It makes my government look bad. You want to use me as a propaganda tool to discourage American soldiers. Forget it.
Zamperini's response angered The Bird even more. The beatings continued.

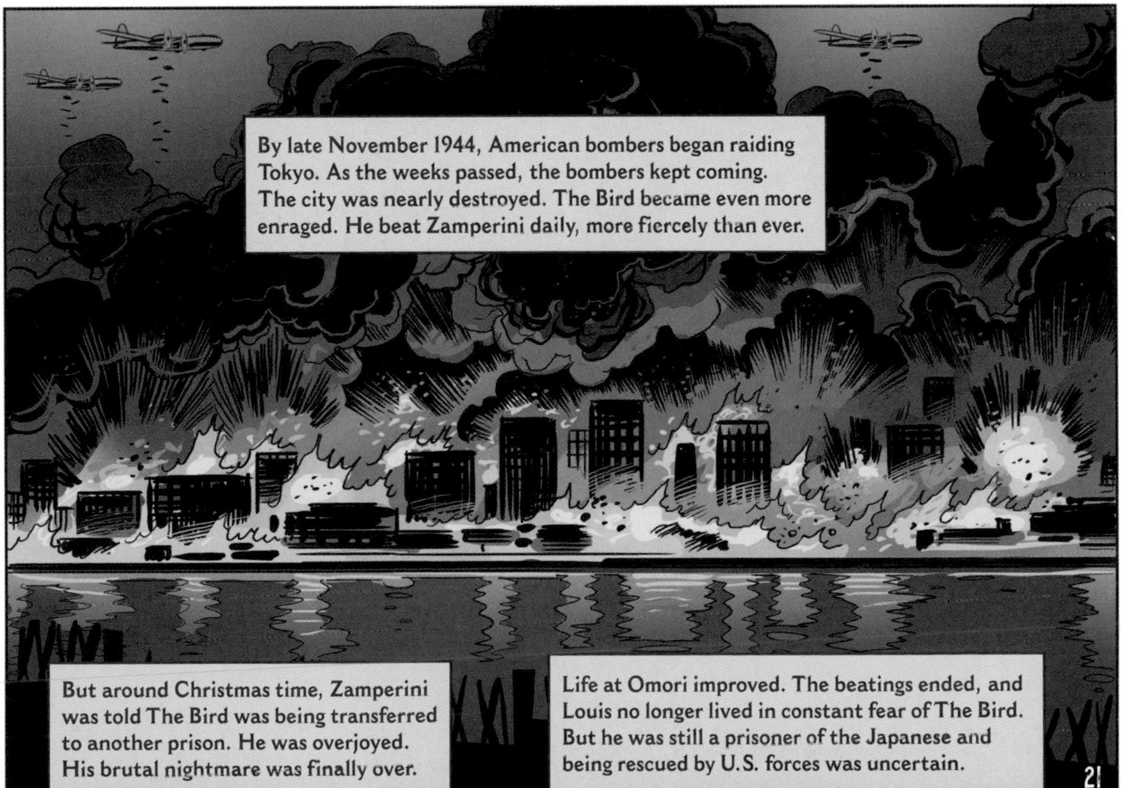
By late November 1944, American bombers began raiding Tokyo. As the weeks passed, the bombers kept coming. The city was nearly destroyed. The Bird became even more enraged. He beat Zamperini daily, more fiercely than ever.
But around Christmas time, Zamperini was told The Bird was being transferred to another prison. He was overjoyed. His brutal nightmare was finally over.
Life at Omori improved. The beatings ended, and Louis no longer lived in constant fear of The Bird. But he was still a prisoner of the Japanese and being rescued by U.S. forces was uncertain.

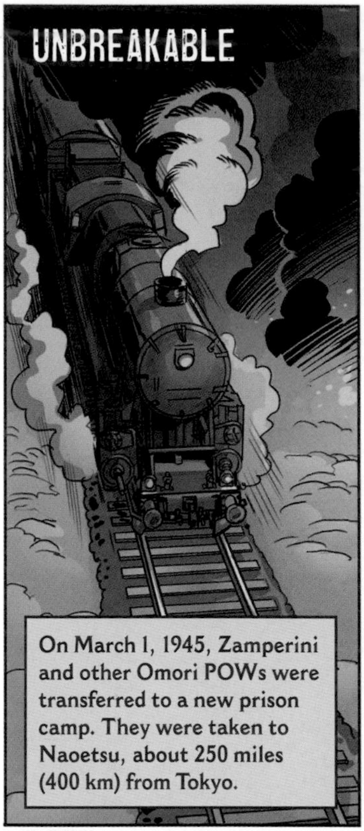
On March 1, 1945, Zamperini and other Omori POWs were transferred to a new prison camp. They were taken to Naoetsu, about 250 miles (400 km) from Tokyo.

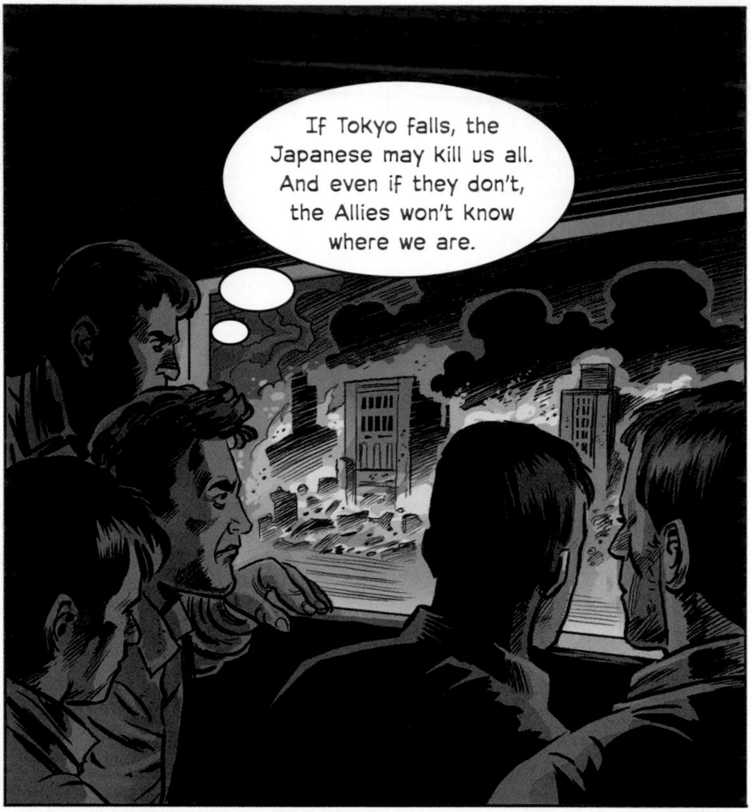
If Tokyo falls, the Japanese may kill us all. And even if they don't, the Allies won't know where we are.

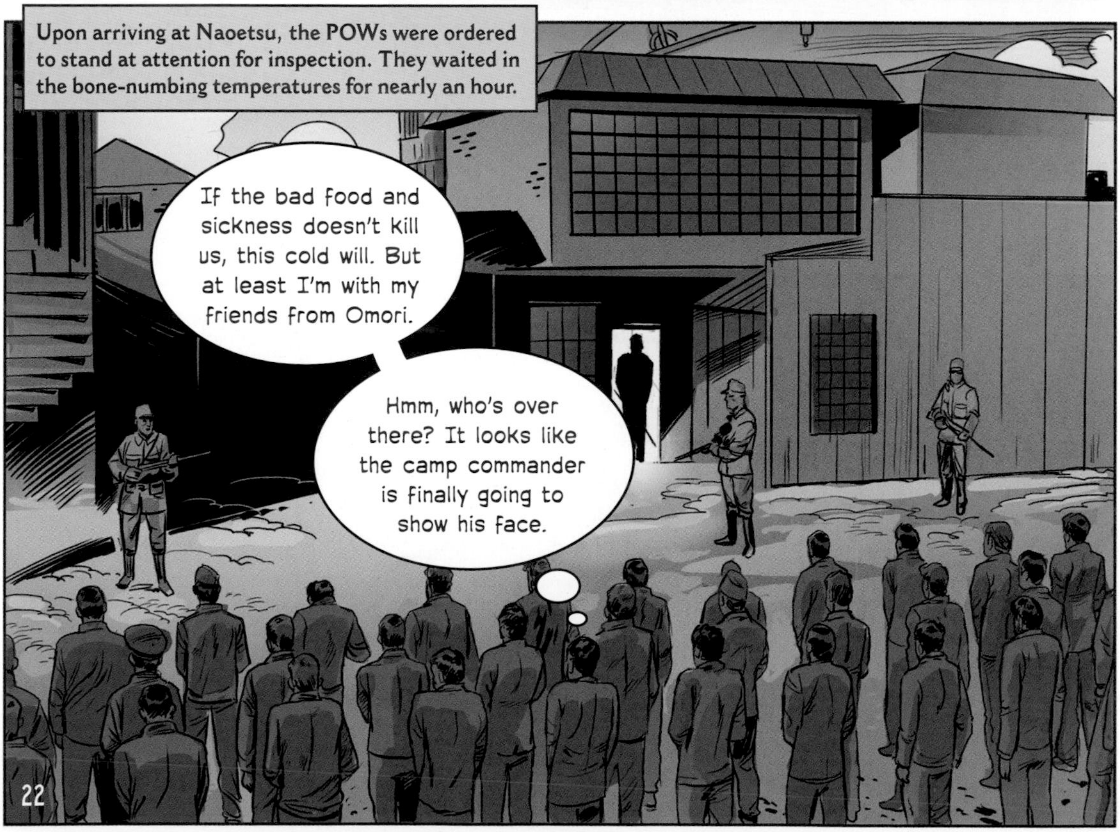
Upon arriving at Naoetsu, the POWs were ordered to stand at attention for inspection. They waited in the bone-numbing temperatures for nearly an hour.
If the bad food and sickness doesn't kill us, this cold will. But at least I'm with my friends from Omori.
Hmm, who's over there? It looks like the camp commander is finally going to show his face.

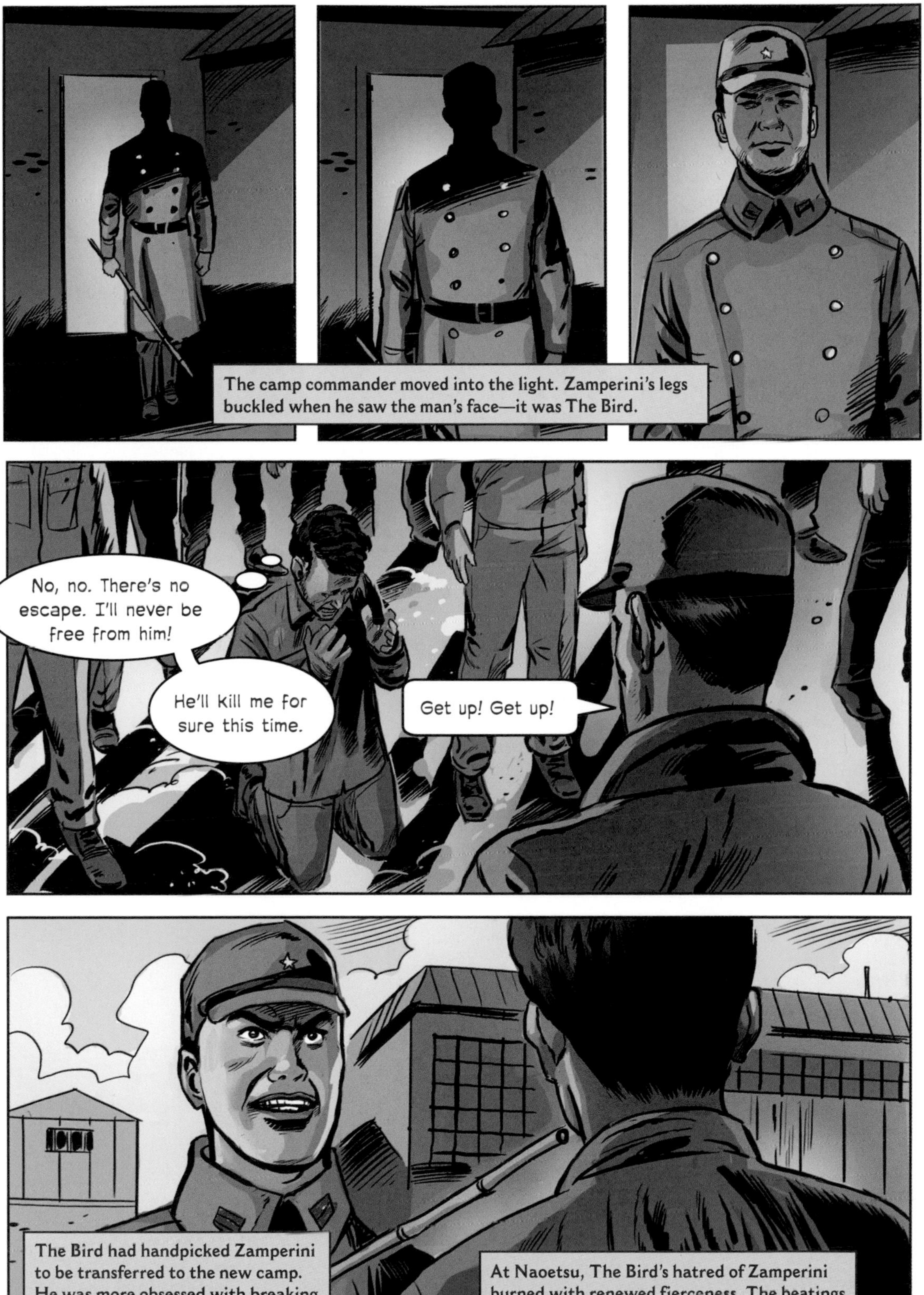
The camp commander moved into the light. Zamperini's legs buckled when he saw the man's face—it was The Bird.
No, no. There's no escape. I'll never be free from him!
He'll kill me for sure this time.
Get up! Get up!
The Bird had handpicked Zamperini to be transferred to the new camp. He was more obsessed with breaking his prisoner than ever.
At Naoetsu, The Bird's hatred of Zamperini burned with renewed fierceness. The beatings resumed—but so did Zamperini's defiance.

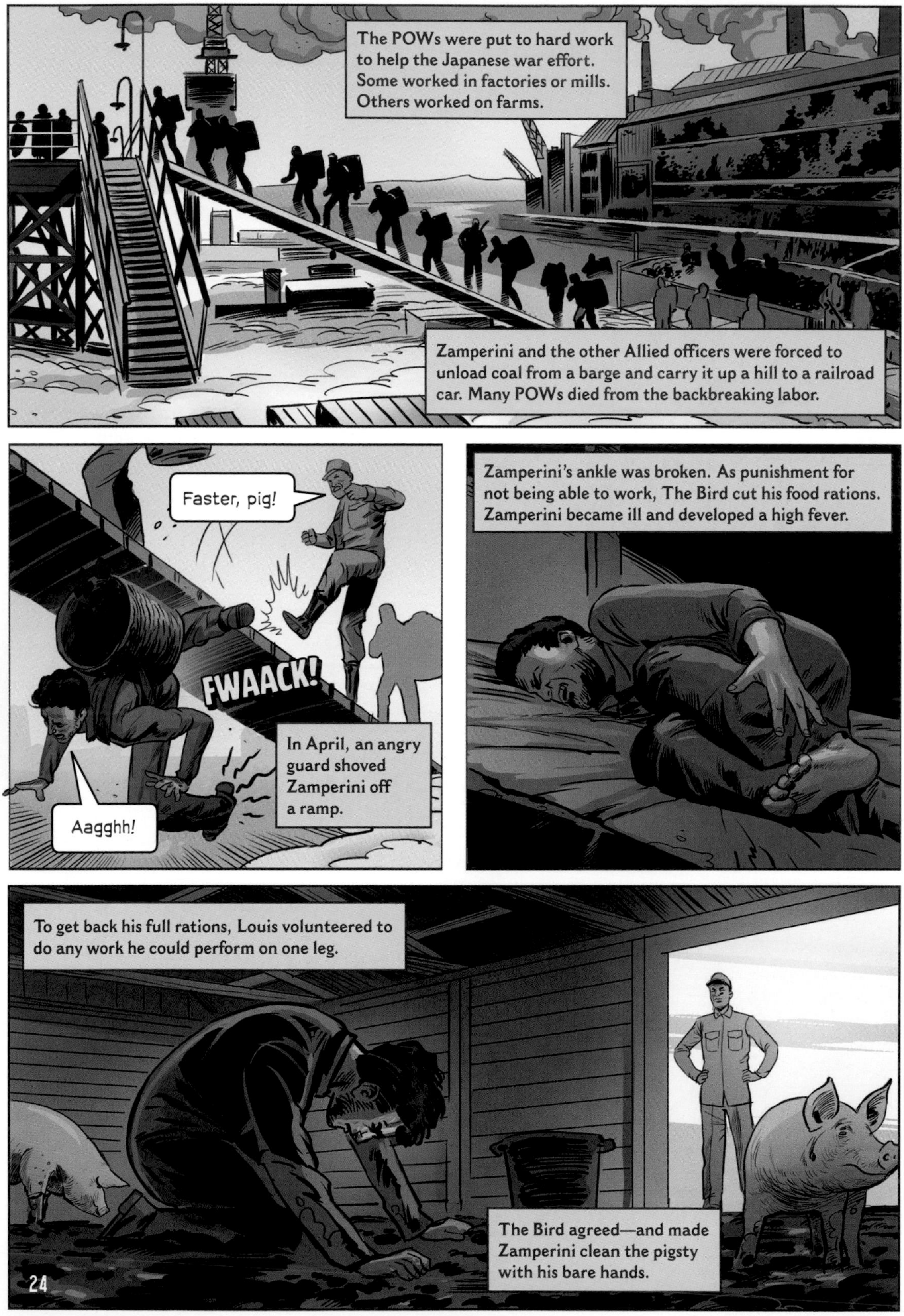

The POWs were put to hard work to help the Japanese war effort. Some worked in factories or mills. Others worked on farms.
Zamperini and the other Allied officers were forced to unload coal from a barge and carry it up a hill to a railroad car. Many POWs died from the backbreaking labor.
Faster, pig!
FWAACK!
In April, an angry guard shoved Zamperini off a ramp.
Aagghh!
Zamperini's ankle was broken. As punishment for not being able to work, The Bird cut his food rations. Zamperini became ill and developed a high fever.
To get back his full rations, Louis volunteered to do any work he could perform on one leg.
The Bird agreed—and made Zamperini clean the pigsty with his bare hands.

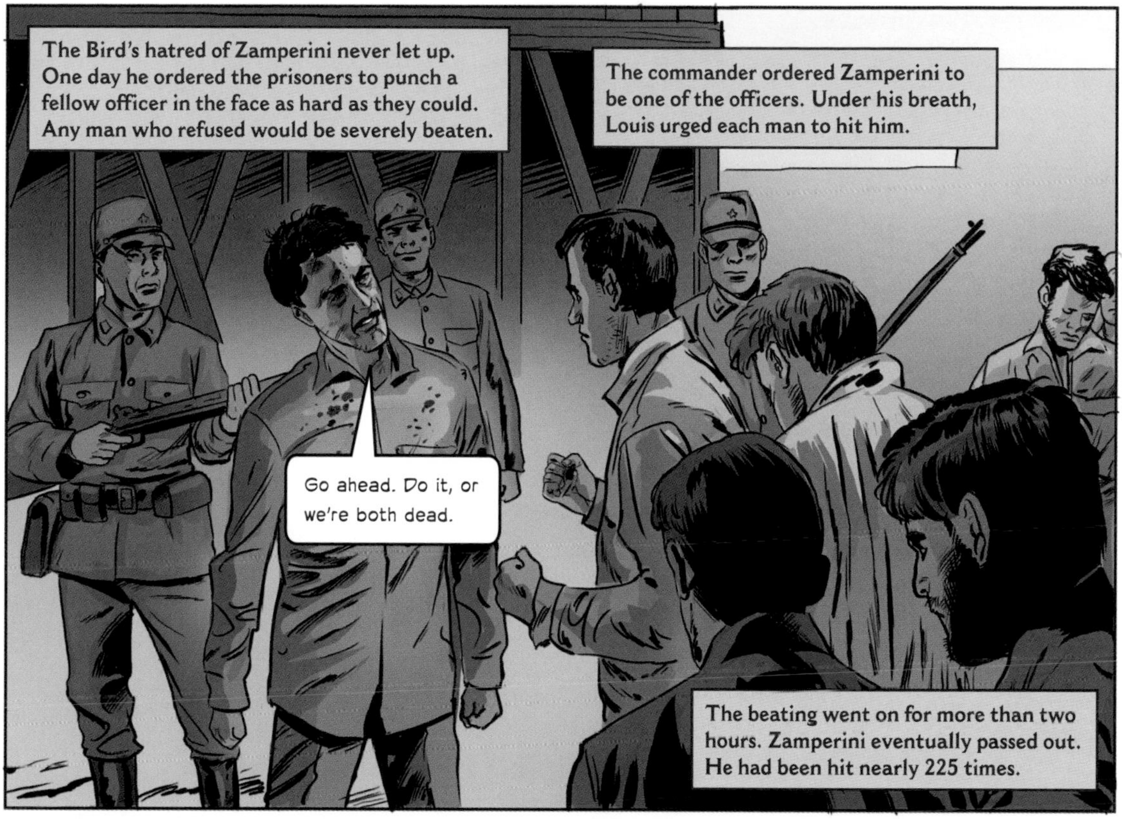
The Bird's hatred of Zamperini never let up. One day he ordered the prisoners to punch a fellow officer in the face as hard as they could. Any man who refused would be severely beaten.
The commander ordered Zamperini to be one of the officers. Under his breath, Louis urged each man to hit him.
Go ahead. Do it, or we're both dead.
The beating went on for more than two hours. Zamperini eventually passed out. He had been hit nearly 225 times.

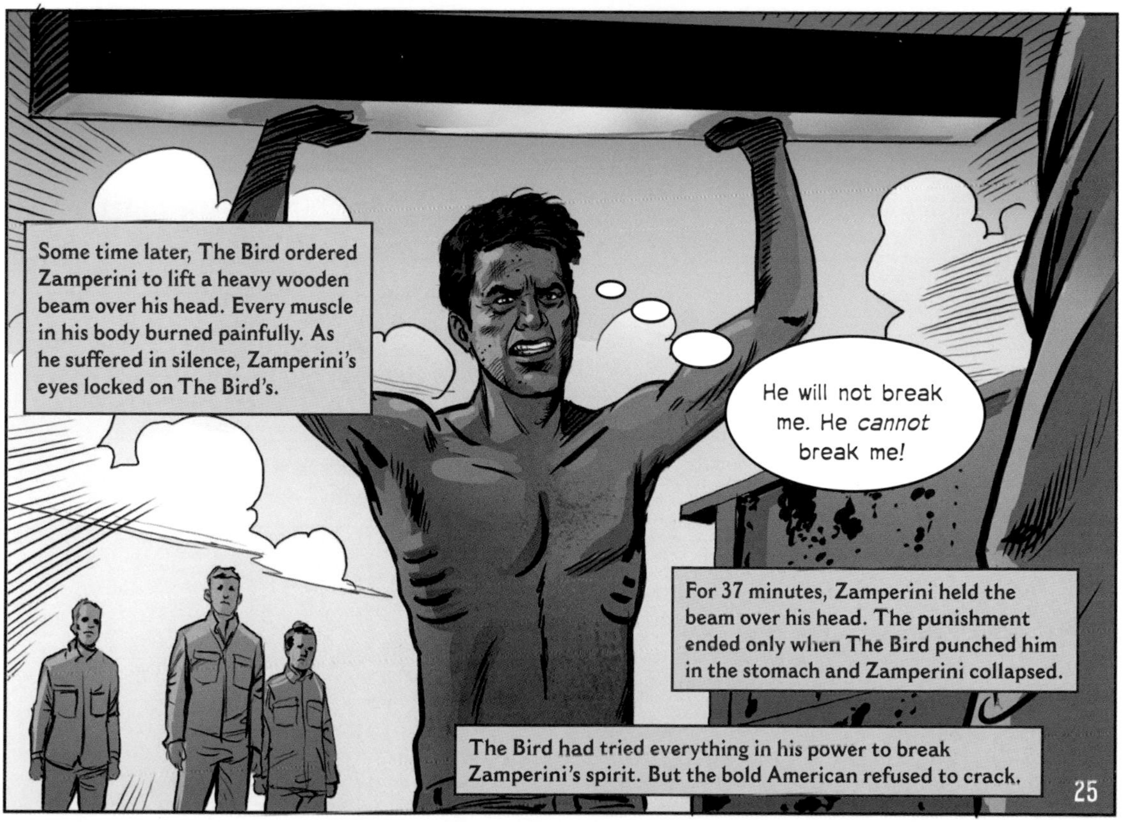
Some time later, The Bird ordered Zamperini to lift a heavy wooden beam over his head. Every muscle in his body burned painfully. As he suffered in silence, Zamperini's eyes locked on The Bird's.
He will not break me. He *cannot* break me!
For 37 minutes, Zamperini held the beam over his head. The punishment ended only when The Bird punched him in the stomach and Zamperini collapsed.
The Bird had tried everything in his power to break Zamperini's spirit. But the bold American refused to crack.

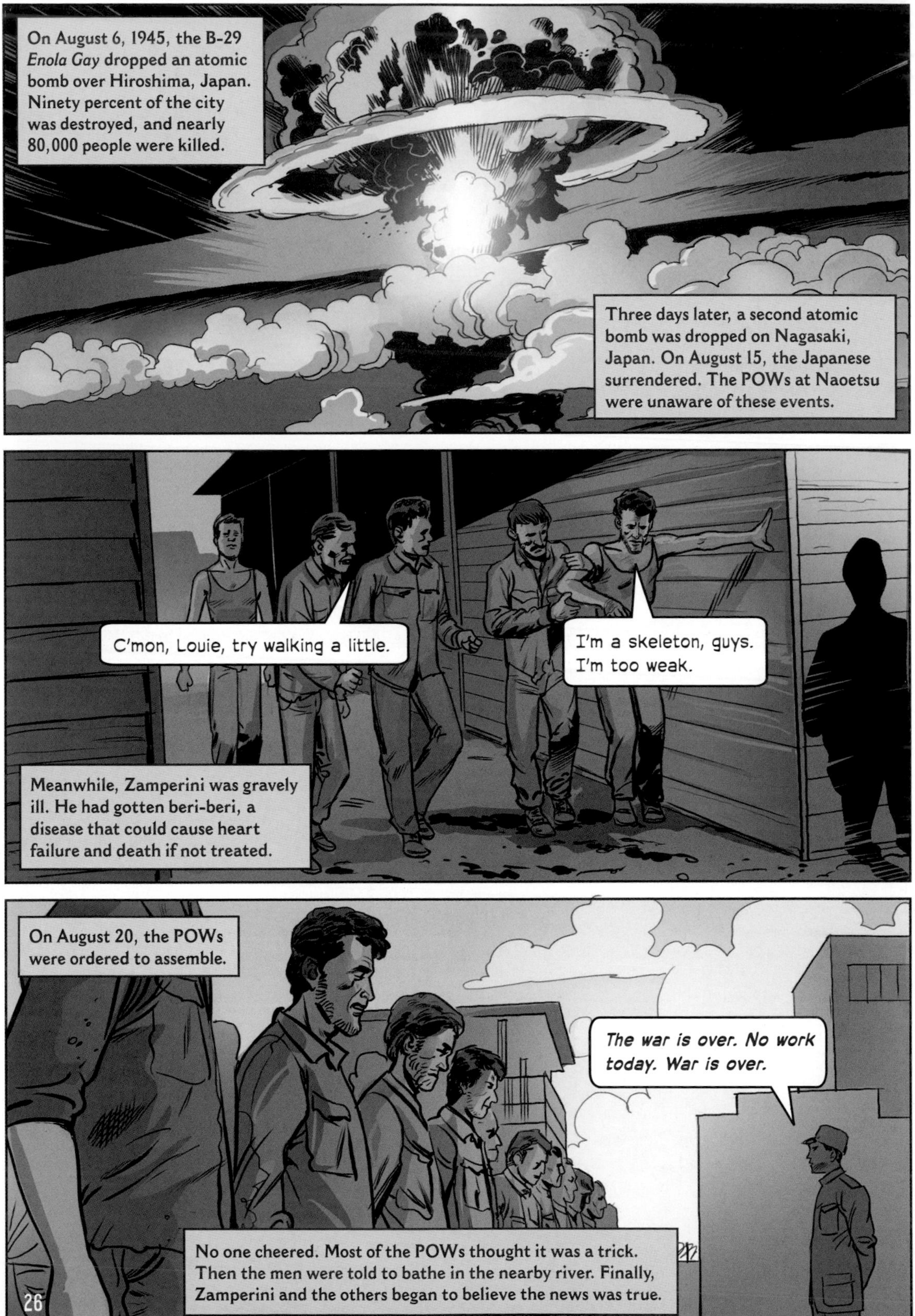
On August 6, 1945, the B-29 *Enola Gay* dropped an atomic bomb over Hiroshima, Japan. Ninety percent of the city was destroyed, and nearly 80,000 people were killed.
Three days later, a second atomic bomb was dropped on Nagasaki, Japan. On August 15, the Japanese surrendered. The POWs at Naoetsu were unaware of these events.
C'mon, Louie, try walking a little.
I'm a skeleton, guys. I'm too weak.
Meanwhile, Zamperini was gravely ill. He had gotten beri-beri, a disease that could cause heart failure and death if not treated.
On August 20, the POWs were ordered to assemble.
The war is over. No work today. War is over.
No one cheered. Most of the POWs thought it was a trick. Then the men were told to bathe in the nearby river. Finally, Zamperini and the others began to believe the news was true.

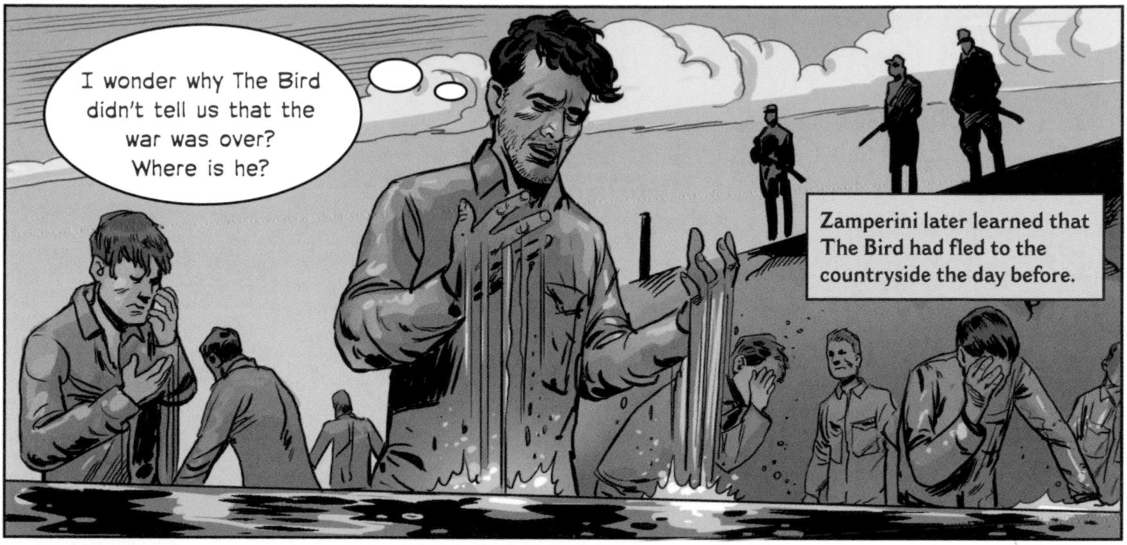
I wonder why The Bird didn't tell us that the war was over? Where is he?
Zamperini later learned that The Bird had fled to the countryside the day before.

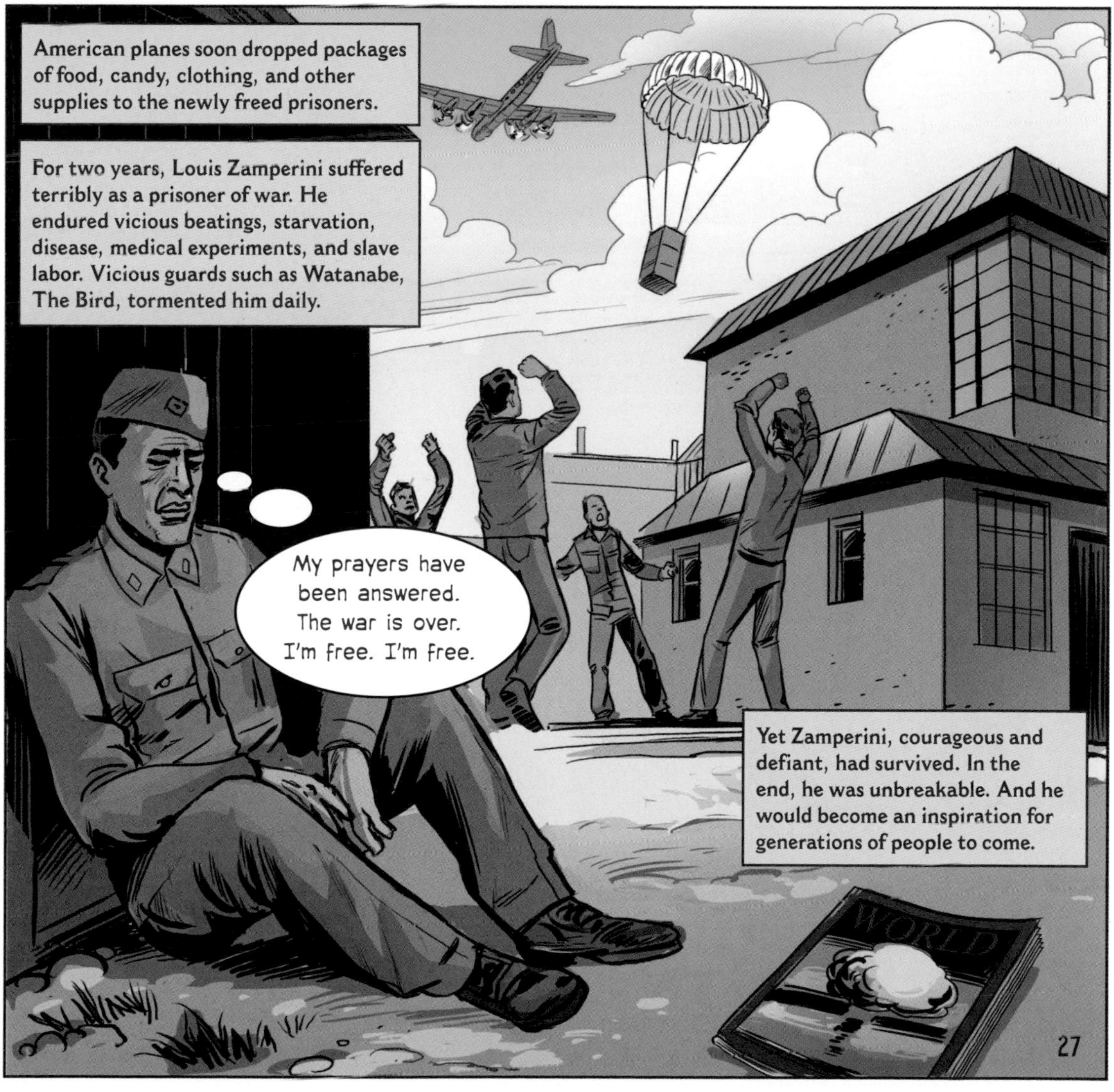
American planes soon dropped packages of food, candy, clothing, and other supplies to the newly freed prisoners.
For two years, Louis Zamperini suffered terribly as a prisoner of war. He endured vicious beatings, starvation, disease, medical experiments, and slave labor. Vicious guards such as Watanabe, The Bird, tormented him daily.
My prayers have been answered. The war is over. I'm free. I'm free.
Yet Zamperini, courageous and defiant, had survived. In the end, he was unbreakable. And he would become an inspiration for generations of people to come.
WORLD

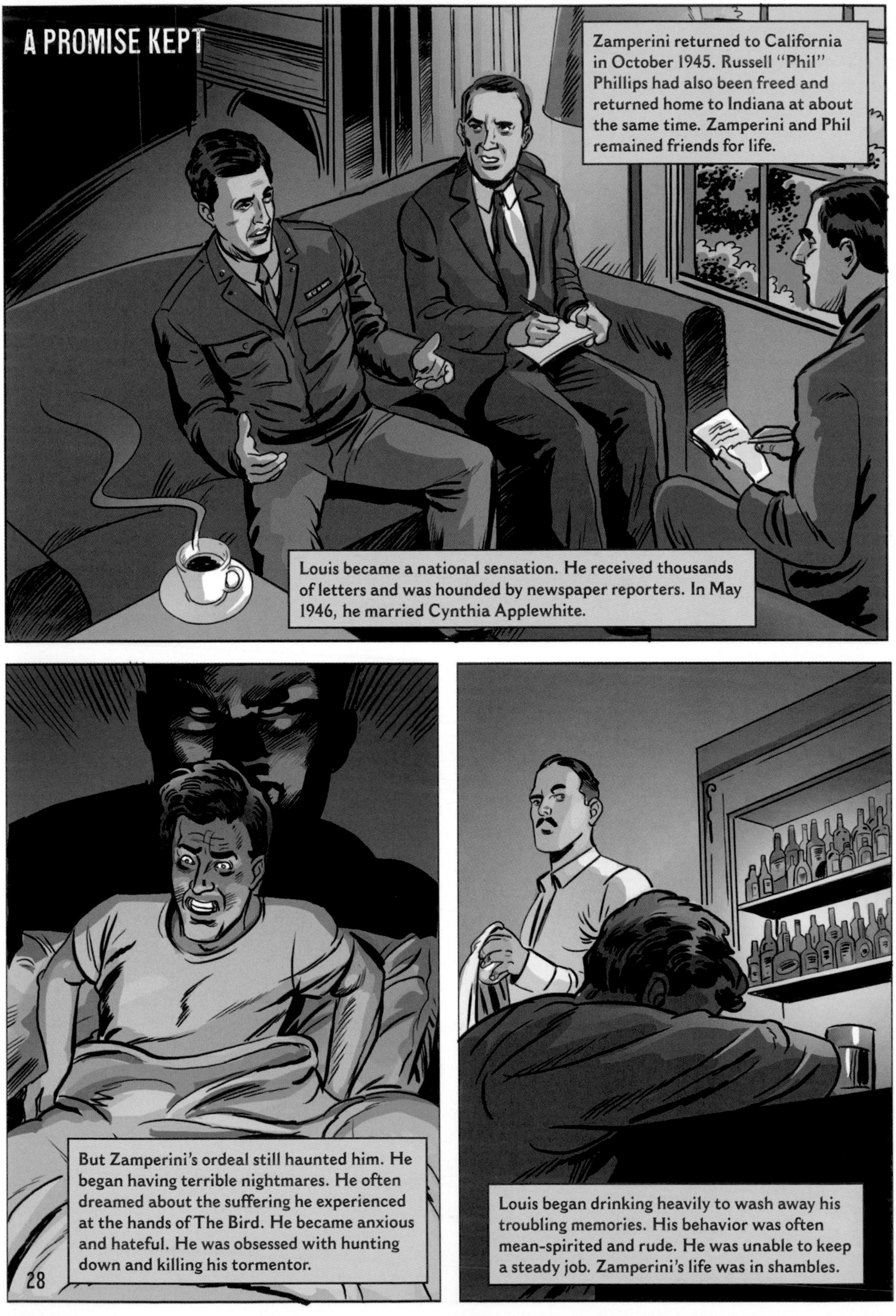
A PROMISE KEPT
Zamperini returned to California in October 1945. Russell "Phil" Phillips had also been freed and returned home to Indiana at about the same time. Zamperini and Phil remained friends for life.
Louis became a national sensation. He received thousands of letters and was hounded by newspaper reporters. In May 1946, he married Cynthia Applewhite.
But Zamperini's ordeal still haunted him. He began having terrible nightmares. He often dreamed about the suffering he experienced at the hands of The Bird. He became anxious and hateful. He was obsessed with hunting down and killing his tormentor.
Louis began drinking heavily to wash away his troubling memories. His behavior was often mean-spirited and rude. He was unable to keep a steady job. Zamperini's life was in shambles.

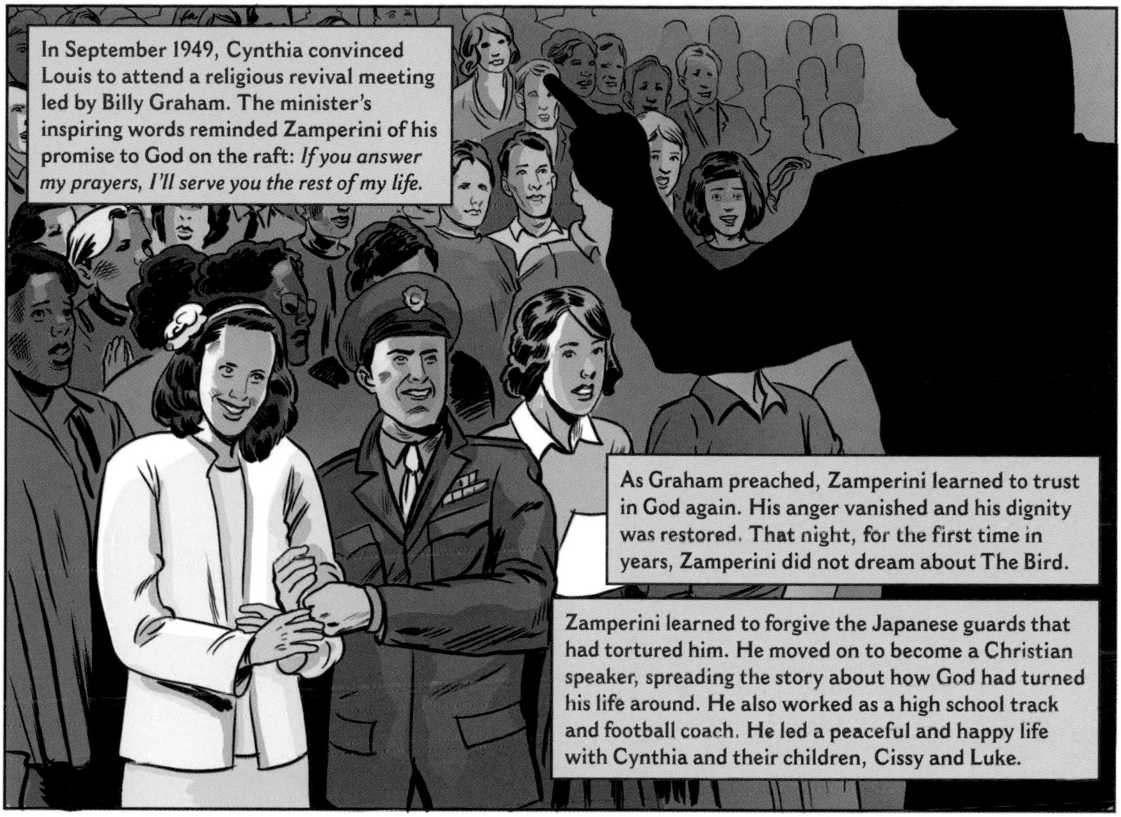
In September 1949, Cynthia convinced Louis to attend a religious revival meeting led by Billy Graham. The minister's inspiring words reminded Zamperini of his promise to God on the raft: *If you answer my prayers, I'll serve you the rest of my life.*
As Graham preached, Zamperini learned to trust in God again. His anger vanished and his dignity was restored. That night, for the first time in years, Zamperini did not dream about The Bird.
Zamperini learned to forgive the Japanese guards that had tortured him. He moved on to become a Christian speaker, spreading the story about how God had turned his life around. He also worked as a high school track and football coach. He led a peaceful and happy life with Cynthia and their children, Cissy and Luke.

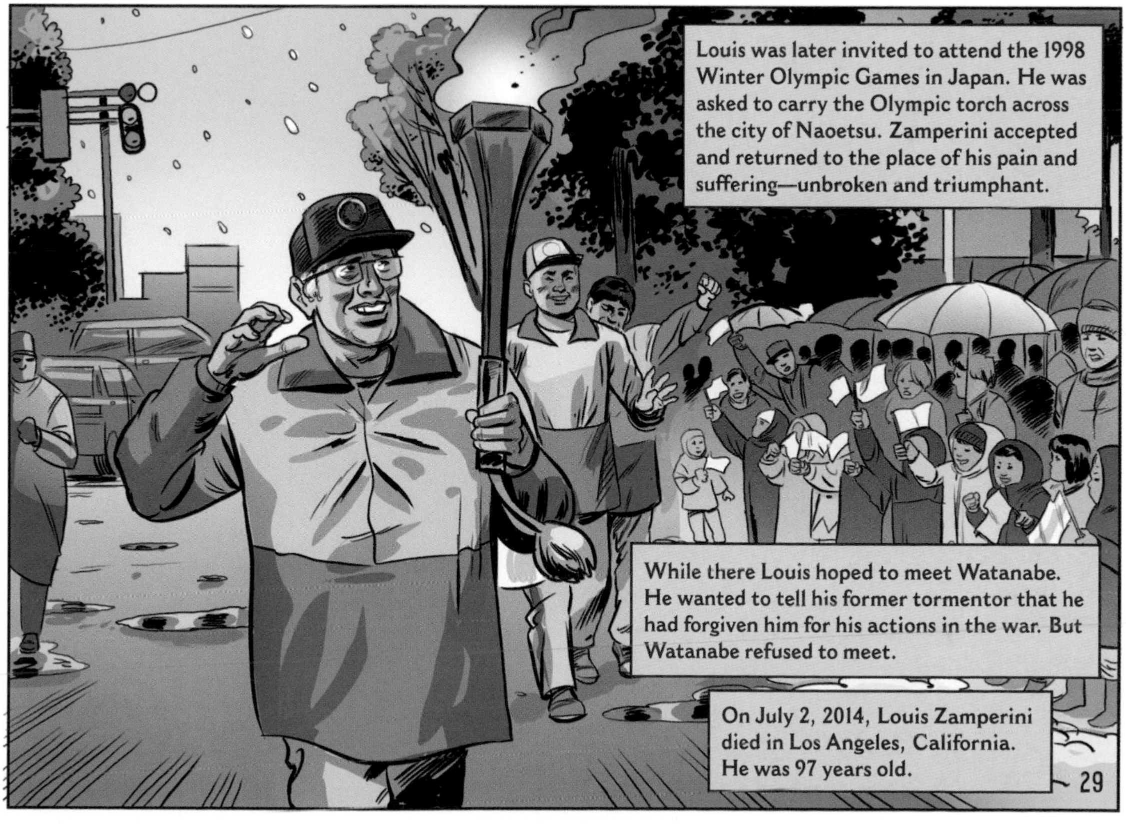
Louis was later invited to attend the 1998 Winter Olympic Games in Japan. He was asked to carry the Olympic torch across the city of Naoetsu. Zamperini accepted and returned to the place of his pain and suffering—unbroken and triumphant.
While there Louis hoped to meet Watanabe. He wanted to tell his former tormentor that he had forgiven him for his actions in the war. But Watanabe refused to meet.
On July 2, 2014, Louis Zamperini died in Los Angeles, California. He was 97 years old.

GLOSSARY

Allies (AL-eyes)—a group of countries that fought together in World War II, including the United States, England, France, and the Soviet Union

bombardier (bahm-buh-DEER)—a bombing crew member who controls where and when bombs drop from airplanes

castaway (KASS-tuh-way)—someone who is lost at sea after a plane or boat wreck

dehydration (dee-hy-DRAY-shuhn)—a life-threatening medical condition caused by a lack of water in the body

dignity (DIG-nuh-tee)—a quality that makes a person worthy of honor or respect

flare gun (FLAIR GUHN)—a handgun that fires a brightly burning object; used as a signal to call for help

humiliation (hyoo-mil-ee-EY-shuhn)—to be made to look or feel foolish or embarrassed

interrogation (in-ter-uh-GEY-shuhn)—the act of questioning someone about things in detail

propaganda (praw-puh-GAN-duh)—information that is spread to try to influence the way people think; often not completely true or fair

sadistic (suh-DIS-tik)—getting pleasure from causing pain, suffering, or humiliation on others

READ MORE

Doeden, Matt. *Surviving a World War II Prison Camp: Louis Zamperini*. They Survived. Minneapolis: Lerner Publications, 2018.

Owens, Lisa L. *Attack on Pearl Harbor*. Heroes of World War II. Minneapolis: Lerner Publications, 2018.

Meloche, Renee Taft. *Louis Zamperini: Survivor and Champion*. Heroes of History for Young Readers. Seattle, WA: Emerald Books, 2014.

CRITICAL THINKING QUESTIONS

- How do you think you would react if you were in Louis Zamperini's place? What would you do during the long months in a prison cell? What would you think about to survive the pain and punishment?

- What do you think Zamperini missed most about his home and family? What would you miss if you were separated from your family and friends in a hostile setting?

- Despite his suffering, Zamperini never lost his dignity. Describe a situation when your self-respect helped you through a difficult time.

INTERNET SITES

History Stories: 8 Things You May Not Know About Louis Zamperini
https://www.history.com/news/8-things-you-may-not-know-about-louis-zamperini

Lucky Louis Zamperini
http://www.americainwwii.com/articles/lucky-louie/

"World War II Isn't Over": Talking to Unbroken Veteran Louis Zamperini
https://www.theatlantic.com/politics/archive/2014/11/world-war-ii-isnt-over-talking-to-unbroken-veteran-louis-zamperini/382616/

INDEX